Critiques of Christianity in African Literature

WITH PARTICULAR REFERENCE TO THE EAST AFRICAN CONTEXT

Edited by

J.N.K. MUGAMBI

East African Educational Publishers

Published by
East African Educational Publishers Ltd
Brick Court
Mpaka Road/Woodvale Grove
Westlands
P.O. Box 45314
Nairobi, Kenya

First published 1992

ISBN 9966-46-580-4

Printed by
Kenya Litho Limited
Changamwe Road, P.O. Box 40775
Nairobi, Kenya

CONTENTS

PREFACE

The relationship between Christianity and particular cultures and cults has been a controversial issue since the beginning of the Church. In the New Testament there are accounts of Jesus being criticized for his interaction with 'sinners' and 'outcasts,' such as tax collectors, Samaritans, and Gentiles. His response was that the new community inaugurating the 'kingdom of God' is inclusive and egalitarian. Whoever would wish to be leader in that 'kingdom' must be willing to be a follower. Whoever would like to be master must be willing to be a servant (Mark 9:33-37; Matthew 5-7).

During the apostolic period the Church was gripped by a fierce controversy as to which cultural identity the ecclesiastical community should adopt, Jewish or Gentile. Although the first Christians were Jews, the Church increasingly attracted many converts from the entire Mediterranean region. Some of the Jewish Christians assumed that since the Christian faith was a direct off-shoot from Judaism and the founder was a Jew, Christianity should maintain a Jewish cultural outlook. Paul and Barnabas, who were widely exposed to non-Jewish culture, religion and philosophy during their missionary endeavours, managed to convince the Judaisers that the Church was not merely a new Jewish party but a new movement altogether. (In India, a similar process took place with regard to Buddhism, Jainism and Sikhism in relationship with Hinduism.) According to the consensus reached at the Ecumenical Council of Jerusalem (Acts 15 and Galatians chapters 2 and 3), everyone could uphold his or her own culture and remain a Christian in full communion with fellow Christians of other cultures with mutual appreciation and respect. Thus in the apostolic Church, after the Council of Jerusalem, there was no demand on Gentile Christians to adopt the norms of the Jewish Christians, even though their evangelization had been facilitated primarily by Jewish apostles.

In the history of the Chuch worldwide, this principle has been honoured more in default than application. Roman missionaries imposed Roman culture on central, northern and western Europe. The Church became the guardian and manifestation of the Roman Empire in the whole of Europe until the sixteenth century. The European Renaissance, reacting against the ascendancy of Islamic civilization in Europe, built its ideology on the cultural achievements of ancient Greece and Rome, which had been bequeathed to contemporary Europeans by Roman, Jewish and Islamic scholars. In the European Reformation, the reformers within various countries re-asserted the cultures of their ethnic communities against the domination of Roman Catholicism. But they articulated their protests in Latin, while promoting their local languages for Bible study and also for the expression of their faith and liturgy. The invention of the printing press greately facilitated this cultural liberation.

When the modern missionary enterprise introduced Christianity from Europe to tropical Africa, this drama of domination and protest was played all over again. Missionaries from Europe became the guardians and mani-festations of their respective national cultures and agents for the promotion of their respective empires abroad. They enjoyed full citizenship, while their converts were subjects. When Africans resisted colonial domination, the missionary enterprise was also under attack, although a clear distinction was made between the Gospel and the European interpretations of it. Thus Christianity continued to grow in tropical Africa, but the missionary enterprise continued to be criticized.

The resistance to colonial domination in tropical Africa can be likened to the European Renaissance, while the various efforts in the Africanization of Christianity are analogous to the European Reformation. The political and economic movements for self-determination in Africa are only one facet of the struggle for liberation-salvation. The other facet comprises religious, ethical and aesthetic efforts of self-expression. Without the secular Renaissance, the European Reformation would have failed and conversely, the Reformation was the religious front of the European Renaissance. Likewise in Africa, total liberation-salvation will be the culmination of political and economic campaigns on the one hand, and the cultural, religious, ethical and aesthetic endeavours of self-expression, on the other. This insight is discerned from an evaluation of the works of contemporary African scholars and creative writers in general. The authors whose critiques of Christianity are presented in this volume, are illustrative of this general perspective. The book analyses selected texts of East African scholars and creative writers including Okot p'Bitek, Taban Lo Liyong, Ngugi wa Thiong'o, Kabiru Kinyanjui, Odhiambo Okite, Henry Okullu and John S Mbiti. The approach is multi-disciplinary, bringing analytical skills from literature, theology, philosphy, history and anthropology into the explication of contemporary African Christianity.

This book captures the response of Africans to Christianity as it has been introduced by the modern missionary enterprise. In many places the Church has not yet celebrated a centenary; in others Christianity has not even been introduced. Thus in tropical Africa the memories of colonial and missionary domination are still fresh and evident. The critiques in this book are illustrative of this observation. The title of the book presupposes a distinction between written, and other forms of critique. Thus 'literature' has a wider meaning than in written, published fiction. All written material is literature, even though the word has in recent times acquired a narrow connotation. It would be possible, for example, to study critiques of Christianity in African song and dance, drama, architecture and oratory. Almost all the *asomi*(those who have acquired academic schooling to various levels) have had exposure to Christianity, and are acquainted in varying degrees with some aspects of Christian missionary presence in tropical Africa. At the same time, their literacy and analytical skills will have enabled them to read for themselves a wide variety of available published materials on Christianity. It is from this diverse exposure that critiques of Christianity emerge. The book fits into a specific historical period of African response to Christianity and should be read as such. It is intended to be neither exhaustive, nor comprehensive, but illustrative.

ACKNOWLEDGEMENT

I thank all those Church leaders of various denominations, (Africans and others), missionaries, scholars, teachers, tutors, and students who since the early 1970s have shared with me their insights with regard to the past, present and future of Christianity in Africa. In particular, I am grateful to those whose writings form the basis of this book, both for their published works, and their oral contributions through discussions and interviews. They may not recall all the nuances of their expressions, but I took notes with considerable interest. This wide exposure has enabled me to appreciate the complexity of the missionary enterprise, and the intricacies of the African responses to Christianity.

The earliest drafts of the book were completed in the mid-1970s, and have been revised for publication. It is interesting to note, however, that in substance, the various critiques remain relatively plausible as the twentieth century draws to a close and as we prepare to enter the twenty-first. May the reader find satisfaction and encouragement in reading this volume, the writing of which, has been a memorable challenge.

J N K Mugambi,   *Nairobi, 1991*

Chapter One

INTRODUCTORY REMARKS

A spiritual rebirth or regeneration ... must be based on self-knowledge and not self-deception. The view that the African has no sins except those imposed on him by outside forces or their agents in Africa does not do justice to the African himself. It treats him either as a puppet of forces—natural and supernatural—he is unable to understand, or as a semi-god.[1]

Reviewing the Christian Missionary Enterprise

Contemporary East Africans are responding to, and interpreting, the brand of Christianity they have encountered with the realization that the Euro-American Christian missionary enterprise is the largest single factor that has contributed to the disruption of African cultural and religious heritage. This disruption has continued to take place through mission stations, churches and schools, and through various relationships between Church and society. In all these relationships, and in every locality, Christianity has been presented not just as a new way of life, but as a Euro-American way of life.

From the early period of the missionary enterprise, African converts came to understand the Christian way of life as being identical with the norms of conduct set for them by the missionaries who introduced Christianity in each particular locality. The school became the largest single factor that contributed to the spreading of Christianity. This fact led to a situation in which Christianity became a 'classroom religion,' to be practised sometimes and abandoned at other times. John V Taylor, a former missionary to Uganda, sees this as one of the greatest failures in Africa, and explains the consequence of the missionary in the following words, with regard to the penetration of Christianity into African personality:

> This might well be the most terrible failure of the Church in Africa—that it meets people only in their best clothes. Those who can see the children only in their uniforms, the clergy only in their robes, the ordinary people only in some 'Christian' context, are unlikely to

> plan or preach or legislate with much wisdom or relevance. Such
> Christianity becomes something to be put on at certain times and in
> particular circumstances, and has nothing to do with other areas of life.[2]

John Taylor, as well as other missionaries, is aware that academic education in Africa, although it served as an instrument for spreading Christianity and Western culture, at the same time distorted the essence of Christianity, because Africans experienced a dichotomy between what they learned at school, and the socialized life that they lived at home. Whereas academic learning emphasized individual performance assessed through graded examinations, the African social life at home was based on human relationships that went beyond the conjugal family, and in which the individual understood himself only in his relationship with his community.

Roland Oliver has observed that since around 1920 the academically educated people have increasingly become critical of the Church as it was propagated in East Africa by missionaries and their African agents. Academically educated Africans have been increasingly unwilling to become actively involved in the activities of the East African Church. This study has sought to investigate some of the main reasons why there has been this reluctance. The majority of Africans have continued to experience a dichotomy between what they learn at school and what they experience in their social life out of school. What they learn at school is not enforced at home, but is often in conflict with their cultural and religious heritage. Christianity belongs more to their academic learning than to their ordinary life at home. For many centuries in Europe this was not the case. The school tried to endorse or develop what the children experienced at home. But in tropical Africa:

> The advance of the Christian Church . . . has depended more upon her
> virtual monopoly of Western education than upon any other factor. Today
> secular governments are taking that monopoly from her and it is a bitter
> irony that the factor which seemed to be Christianity's greatest strength in
> Africa threatens to prove its heaviest liability. For to a great extent, it
> (Christianity) has become a classroom religion.[3]

It is in this setting that East Africans respond to Christianity today. But why should those who have gone through the mission schools and through a systematized indoctrination against their own heritage and in favour of an alien culture, reject what they have received and strive to affirm their disrupted heritage? Ali Mazrui, one of the contemporary highly educated East Africans, answers this question by asserting that **the spread of Christianity did not succeed in destroying or distorting all the African values:**

> Aesthetic values are often the most conservative of all values in their
> response to foreign influence. It is often far easier to be converted to the
> ethics of a conquering power, than to the aesthetics. An African is often

more easily converted to Western Christianity than to Western classical music. And the chances are that even formal monogamy will become part of African life sooner than we expect high Western opera or the ballet to enter the lives of African peoples. As between societies which are otherwise very different, agreement between right and wrong, good and bad, is often easier to achieve than agreement on what is beautiful and what is ugly. That may perhaps be one reason, among many, as to why black people have already produced three winners of the Nobel Prize for Peace, and not a single Miss World.[4]

Mazrui's observation seems convincing, and if it is a correct one, it may explain why the most vocal East African critics against Christianity, as it was established by the Euro-American missionary enterprise, have been creative writers, poets, painters—artists in general. This study has shown this to be the case. Apparently, there are more outspoken artists who are openly against Christianity than there are educated Africans of other disciplines.

East African artists have expressed their indignation against the humiliating and even degrading process that was used by the missionary enterprise to Christianize Africa. Some East Africans have warned against an over reaction to colonial and missionary experiences, because such over reactions may emphasize the blame on the foreigners without encouraging contemporary East Africans to make a self-criticism that will enable them to create new insights and genius to enable them build a new future. Bethwel Ogot, a prominent East African historian, emphasized his caution as follows:

> I have pleaded for a more realistic treatment of the African not as a special species with common characteristics, but as a normal human being. I have further suggested that in order to do this effectively, we must examine our presuppositions primarily as a path-clearing operation, and as a means of avoiding the kind of over-simplifications and over-generalizations which have bedevilled our literature. I am certain that if we do this, we shall discover that the African has not only been sinned against, but that he too, has been a sinner. And it is on the basis of such a discovery that we can inaugurate a true generation.[5]

These are valuable words of advice, which ought to be taken seriously by every academically educated contemporary East African. East African literature, both creative and historical, is characterized by complaints against the way in which Africans were mistreated during the colonial period. The collaboration between the missionary societies and the imperial powers is almost everywhere spelt out. However, Ogot's caution emphasizes that East Africans need to move from mere blames on colonial rulers and foreign missionaries to a self-criticism that will enable them to generate, from within themselves, an internal dynamic to enable East Africa to make creative contributions for itself, for the whole continent of Africa, and for the world as a whole. Without self-analysis and self-criticism, such creative genius and insights will not emerge from the consciousness of East African artists, historians, theologians, and so on.

This study, in bringing together the reflections of contemporary East Africans with regard to Christianity, is a contribution towards this self-analysis, self-criticism and self-knowledge. It is only a preliminary study, and hopefully, more Africans will take up the challenge of continuing the discussion using this approach, so that they can influence the reflections of each other, for the sake of a growing discourse.

Aylward Shorter, with his deep interest in seeing Christianity firmly rooted in Africa, realizes that his hope will not be realized until Africans themselves begin to defend Christianity in Africa. Until now Christianity in East Africa has been defended mainly by missionaries. Hence he challenges East African Christians to engage themselves in the development of African Christian theology. Such a theology will ultimately have to be the product of African thought and experience. In Shorter's view:

> It belongs primarily to the Africans themselves to say what their contribution might contain. At the moment it is almost impossible to know what African theologians themselves think. Their theses lie scattered in university libraries of Europe and America, and nothing has been done to bring them together, to compare and analyse them and to discern the trends of thought they represent. It is perhaps unlikely that these works would betray much homogeneity. Their authors have not been able to influence each other, and many, if not most, have not been permitted to break free of European theological traditions and styles. What we are now awaiting is an independent and original contribution from Africa itself. There are signs that it is on the horizon . . .[6]

This study has attempted to provide a preliminary analysis of what East Africans think of Christianity. Though it has not dealt with the theses of East African theologians which are 'stored in archives and libraries abroad,' it has provided a starting point from which further analysis may be made. It is important to add to Shorter's challenges, however, that African Christian theology must reflect not only what African Christians think, but is must also take account of the criticisms of non-Christian East Africans. Only by so doing will it be making a constructive contribution to the future of religion in Africa.

East African Creative Writers

In general, this study has led to the conclusion that the East African creative writers have challenged the theological assumptions that for a long time have been held and maintained by most missionaries and their African converts in the established churches. African Christians in churches founded by the missionary agencies almost always adopted the theological assumptions of the missionaries who introduced Christianity to them.

One such assumption was that missionaries were nearer to God and Heaven than Africans.[7] This was an assumption that the missionaries brought with them in their interpretation of the Great Commission to go to all the corners of the world and preach the Gospel to every creature. The assumption had the effect of endorsing a master-servant relationship between the missionaries and their African converts. The relationship was reinforced by the colonial rule, which justified Euro-American domination over Africans on the ground that Europe and North America, being Christian continents, held the monopoly of the mission to Christianize and Civilize the rest of the world, Africa included.

This assumption was challenged by African Christian and non-Christian pioneers of liberation struggles all over the continent.. The independent churches sought to challenge the monopoly of European and North American missionaries to interpret the Christian scriptures, while politicians challenged the monopoly of European Imperial Powers to determine the political and economic destiny of African peoples. The negritude school in French-speaking Africa sought to challenge Euro-American cultural, superiority, by claiming a distinct African personality which had to be recognized before Africans could make a notable contribution to the universal culture which each imperial power claimed to be building. It is, therefore, not surprising that the independent church movements and the negritude school of thought, often coincided with the African struggles for political and economic liberation.

Another assumption was that there was nothing valuable in African cultural and religious heritage, and that the African background must be ignored or abandoned by any African who chose to become a Christian.[8] This assumption led to the conclusion that the European cultural tradition, by virtue of its long influence by Christianity, was itself Christian, whereas African culture was pagan, heathen and primitive. In the contemporary East African context, this assumption has led to the hesitation and widespread refusal by many missionaries and African Christians to take African religions seriously, for fear of syncretism. The debate for and against the teaching of traditional African religion in East African schools has been precipitated by this assumption. Many African and foreign Christians have erroneously assumed that Christianity, as it was introduced by the missionary enterprise, was pure, without any non-Christian elements from pagan Europe.

However, many of the customs now accepted as Christian, such as Easter, Christmas and Christian Marriage, were developed in Europe through a process of Christianizing pagan customs. The fixing of Christmas and Easter calendars, for example, was determined more by European pagan religious customs than by historical considerations of the birth and crucifixion of Jesus. In that sense, Christianity was full of syncretism even before it reached East Africa through the missionary enterprise.

Furthermore, African Christians have been taught to embrace Christianity as a culture, rather than a challenge to every culture. Thus they were led to assume that there was a radical difference between 'Christian life' and traditional African life.[9] Although it is true that every committed Christian is called by Christian scriptures to distinguish himself from those who are not Christians, this distinction has in practice been interpreted to imply a distinction between those who have accepted norms set up by the missionaries and those who have rejected such norms and chosen to live according to their cultural and religious heritage. Those who have rejected acculturation have been looked down upon as being enemies of Christianity and civilization. Ngugi's novels and Okot p'Bitek's poems have concentrated on challenging this assumption, and showing that in spite of the apparent inadequacies the African way of life provided coherent answers to the religious quest of Africans in their tradition life. Christian life and European life have been assumed to be one and the same thing, but the academically educated East Africans, having experienced the distinction between the two on the one hand, and their own heritage on the other, have challenged this assumption vehemently.

African Scholars who are committed or sympathetic to Christianity now argue that if the Christian Gospel cannot speak directly to Africans in their own cultural and religious context, its claim to be universal cannot be sustained. A few Christians all over the contemporary world have realized the falsehood of this assumption, and have begun to advocate Contextual Christian Theology. This new interpretation of Christianity has not been fully accepted by all Christians and this fact still makes it difficult for academically educated East African critics to accept Christianity as a universal religion. The Christians who are opposed to Contextual Theology argue that such a development will destroy the universality of the Church, while its advocates argue that the Gospel can, and will be, meaningful only if it is relevant to each particular social, political and economic situation. Jesus was very contextual in His teaching and, therefore, Christianity will be meaningful only if it is contextual to every individual and community. Hence Contextual Theology will affirm the universality of the Gospel rather than deny it.

Yet another assumption is connected with the understanding of the Biblical message. Since the establishment of the Bible Canon, the Bible has been accepted in the Christian Church as the Inspired and Infallible Word of God. For many Christians, inspiration and infallibilty of the Bible have meant that the Christian scriptures are a manual to be followed word for word, and to be applied to every situation irrespective of the social or historical context. Fundamentalism is a widespread assumption in contemporary East Africa, and it provides a strong case for critics against Christianity. The debate between Micere Githae Mugo and Carl McIntire in 1975 illustrates the scandal which fundamentalism showers upon the Christian Gospel.[10]

The failure of many East African Christians to accept that the Bible was written at particular historical contexts, dealing with particular social and religious issues, leads the critics to conclude that if the fundamentalists are right in their views, then the Bible is irrelevant in contemporary East Africa. However, other Christians, such as Henry Okullu and Burgess Carr, consider the Bible to be a guidebook that provides divine insights for determining the lines of action at any given contextual situation. The so-called Bible-believing Christians have regarded the Bible as a blueprint to be followed literally in all ages and for all situations. This view has made East African Christianity very vulnerable to its critics. Nevertheless, the Ecumenical Movement, which fundamentalists attack vehemently, has tried very hard to establish the balance between Christian Faith and corresponding social commitment, which is lacking in contemporary fundamentalism.

The Roman Catholic Church now recognizes the necessity of interpreting the Christian Gospel in terms that are relevant and meaningful in each particular context. Since the Second Vatican Council, much progress has been made in this direction, and Catholic Christians now have the Scriptures available in their vernaculars. Languages other than Latin have been accepted for use in the Liturgy, and some aspects of traditional African worship are being appropriated to Christian worship.[11] All these efforts are being made in the endeavour to establish Christianity firmly in Africa, and in order that Jesus Christ may be incarnate in contemporary Africa.

In this endeavour, the churches established by the Euro-American missionary enterprise have a great deal to learn from the indigenous African Christian churches, to whom the incorporation of African culture in worship is common and natural.

East African Scholars

Okot p'Bitek has been one of the most outspoken critics of Christianity in contemporary East Africa. He has noted a distinction between the teaching of Joshua, the Messiah (Jesus Christ) and that of Saul of Tarsus (St. Paul). He emphasizes that it was Paul's moral code that became the basis of Euro-Christian morality, which has been imposed upon the peoples of East Africa through the missionary enterprise. In Okot's view, it was Paul's hatred of sex, rather than Christ's more humane attitude to women, that became the basis of Christian morality.[12]

Okot's distinction between the teachings of Jesus and Paul is interesting, though he has not made a systematic analysis of the two in relation to contemporary East Africa. There are other points at which Paul seems to have shifted the emphasis of the teaching of Jesus. Paul's doctrine of Justification by Faith, which became central to

Prostestant Theology, tended to overlook the teaching of Jesus that not every one who calls him 'Lord, Lord' will enter the Kingdom of God, but everyone who does His will.

.The formation of Christianity as a religion separate from Judaism and in confrontation with Graeco-Roman heritage, was the work of Paul and his followers rather than the work of Jesus, although Paul claimed his authority from his conversion and commitment to Iesus Christ. Most of the theological books of the New Testament are ascribed to Saul of Tarsus, who after persecuting Christians became the greatest architect and advocate of what Okot p'Bitek calls the 'cult of Christ,' especially in the Graeco-Roman areas.

Apparently, Jesus did not organize his followers into a Church or a political party, although he had twelve disciples whom he occasionally sent out to preach his message. Paul, on the other hand, was very concerned about the growth of the Churches started by him and his followers. It would be interesting to make a detailed study of Jesus and Paul, but that is not the objective of the present concern here.

Okot raises several points in his criticisms against Christianity as it was introduced and propagated in East Africa. Neither the Protestant nor the Catholic missionary endeavour is exempted from this criticism. One of the points about which Okot is concerned, is theological. He accuses some African Christian Scholars, such as John S Mbiti of dressing up African deities with Hellenic robes and parading them before the Western world. According to Okot, many of the African Christian scholars have been writing mainly to Europeans, trying to convince the unbelieving Western world and African peoples were as 'civilized' as Western people.

Mbiti has replied to this accusation by emphasizing that in his works, he has tried to use categories and terms which are understandable, and that most of the terms he uses are derived from the traditional African attributes of God, about which Okot seems very concerned. In response to Okot's criticism, Mbiti has remarked that these categories are not his own inventions, he has simplified and classified them for academic purposes. 'The terms used for classification could of course, be different, but I had to use some terms.'[13]

Thus Mbiti suggests that the usage of common theological terms does not necessarily imply 'Hellenization of African deities. Okot does not approve of an approach in which African religions are studied in comparison or contrast with Christianity. He insists that African religions should be studied as they are all in their own right. Okot's criticism would probably fall more heavily on such an approach as that of Malcolm McVeigh in *God in Africa: Conceptions of God in African Traditional Religions and Christianity*. In this book, McVeigh concentrates on the study of African Traditional Religion using criteria from Christian theology as they were discerned by Edwin Smith. The main chapter of the book deals with questions about God which, in Christian theology, are positively answered, but in African Traditional Religion receive negative or vague answers. The following are the questions McVeigh asks:

Personality	:	Is God a Person?
Monotheism	:	Is God One?
Disposition	:	Does God Love Man?
Revelation	:	Does God Reveal Himself?
Ethics	:	Does God Require Righteousness?
Worship	:	Is God Worshipped?[14]

For Christianity, these questions are answered in strong affirmatives, but for African religions that is not the case. Okot criticizes this approach because it analyses African Traditional Religion on the basis of questions which Africans themselves do not normally ask, and according to criteria of judgement which are not characteristic to African religious thought.

The conclusion of McVeigh, and of Edwin Smith,[15] is that Christianity has a contribution to make to the African Religious thought. But their assessment of that contribution is based on those external criteria, and this seems to be Okot's concern. According to this approach, African Traditional Religion remains incomplete, until the Christian contribution is introduced. Mbiti's studies have forwarded the observation that Africans in traditional life 'pay more attention to two dimensions of time (Zamani, and Sasa) than they do to other dimensions (future).' It seems to him that Christianity has helped Africans to develop growing emphasis on the future dimension. Though this is one of Mbiti's original contributions in the study of African Religion, it seems that Okot p'Bitek would still question the approach because it still analyses African religious thought in relation to Christianity. Okot suggests that the role of the African scholar ought to be two-fold:

First, to expose and destroy all false ideas about African peoples and culture that have been perpetuated by Western scholarship. Vague terms ... must be subjected to critical analysis and thrown out or redefined to suit African interests. Second, the African scholar must endeavour to present the institutions of African peoples as they really are. Western scholars, had to justify the colonial system, hence the need for the myth of the 'primitive.' The African has nothing of the sort to justify. [16]

Along the direction of study he has proposed, Okot p'Bitek has published a book on the *Religion of the Central Luo*, in which he records the religious heritage of this people from their own perspective. In his view, African deities have been described in a biased way because of assumptions deriving from early Western Christian theology. He has listed four basic assumptions that have led to the mistakes he urges African scholars to correct. The first assumption is that the world has a purpose, and that everything in the universe was created to serve either an internal purpose or an external one, or both. He traces this assumption to the theology of Thomas Aquinas, and particularly to his 'Fifth Proof' of the existence of God. Thomas Aquinas had argued that even listless things serve the purpose of some being outside them, and that being must be God who created them. Against this assumption, Okot has written:

> There is no evidence that African peoples see a purpose in all things. Indeed, most of the religious activities in African religions seem to be part of the ways and means of dealing existing or threatening dangers . . . The purpose of any particular object is determined by its use to human beings, and not of by some being outside them. Even the deities are there to serve the interests of men. The African deities are for man, and not man for them.[17]

The second assumption which Okot has attacked, is that the temporal order of nature is in some sense inferior and illusory. In Okot's opinion, this is the assumption that led Christians to over emphasize other-worldliness in their teaching. It seems that Okot interprets Christianity as if other-worldliness is a dominant doctrine in Western Christianity, even in the contemporary period. Though it was a dominant emphasis in the Medieval and Reformation periods, this doctrine has been challenged greatly during the twentieth century, by Christian theologians in many parts of the world. Many Christian theologians today are emphasizing that Christian Salvation involves the whole person, and not just the soul. Though it is true that there are still some fundamentalist Christian groups that emphasize other-worldliness, it ought to be noted that this view is not accepted by many Christian leaders. Nevertheless, against the assumption, Okot has made this observation:

> It seems that there is no other-worldliness in African religious thought. African ethics is not grounded on a promise or threat by some god that the good people will, in future, enjoy life in heaven, while the bad will cook in a great fire. In this sense, the use of the term heaven in describing African religious concepts is confusing and misleading.[18]

This observation that there is no other-worldliness in African religious thought has been made by other religious thinkers. Kwame Nkrumah, for example, made the observation that the African concept of the universe is monistic, whereas the Euro-Christian concept of the same is dualistic. According to Nkrumah, the monistic concept of the universe is a basic assumption in all traditional African thought, including religious thought. This was one of the major contrasts which Nkrumah noticed between traditional African philosophy and Euro-Christian philosophy. Nkrumah made this observation in *Consciencism*, his proposed philosophy for the total decolonization of Africa.[19] In a different context, John K Agbeti made the same observation, in an analytical essay on African Theology.[20]

The third assumption that Okot suggests ought to be abandoned, is that God is unknowable. He criticizes John Mbiti because Mbiti has apologized to God for attempting to describe Him, and for doing it poorly. In his criticism, Okot has observed that:

> Most African peoples know the names, abode and characteristics of their deities. They know them by the diseases they cause. The task of the diviner is, precisely, to determine which deity is responsible for a particular misfortune, and how to deal with it . . . The knowledge about their deities is not limited, inadequate or ridiculous in any way.[21]

It may be observed here that while Okot is correct in noting that most African peoples know the names and attributes of deities, it is also true that not all African peoples identify their deities according to the diseases they cause, or according to the specialized roles which they hold in the practical daily life of the people. Okot has noted that in northern Uganda certain chiefdom deities are carried from place to place. This is not the case among many other African peoples. Perhaps this is why his insistence that the study of traditional religion in Africa should be done in plural rather than in singular, is significant and important.

The question as to whether the study should be done in singular or in plural has not been conclusively answered. Scholars hold differing views on it. Geoffrey Parrinder and Bolaji Idowu seem to suggest that the study should be studied in singular. Okot p'Bitek and Malcolm McVeigh suggest it should be studied in plural. John Mbiti, on the other hand, seems to have revised his earlier position in which he suggested that the study should be conducted in plural, and, now he accepts both as appropriate approaches to the study of religion in traditional Africa.

The fourth assumption that concerns Okot, is the Christian doctrine of monotheism. In Okot's opinion, this is the most important pitfall for the Christian student of African religions. From this doctrine according to Okot's observation, a further assumption arises, that Africans also must have one God. In attacking this assumption, he launched his heaviest criticism of John S Mbiti, who in *Concepts of God in Africa* has observed that in general, Africans are monotheistic.

The last and most important pitfall for the Christian student of African Traditional Religions is the belief in one God, and the assumption which arises, from it, namely that Africans must also have a High God. It is this assumption which has led Evans-Pritchard to interpret the numerous deities of the Nuer as *refractions* of God; and Placide Tempels to arrange the so-called 'life-forces' of the Bantu in a hierarchy at the apex of which is the supposed High God. This also explains the pre-occupation of many writers with some 'half-forgotten deities which are described as no longer interested in the affairs of men and yet, they are called High God.'[22]

It seems from this quotation that Okot p'Bitek accepts to a limited extent the observation of some Christian scholars that African deities are 'no longer interested in the affairs of men.' But he explains this disinterest not in terms of 'the god or gods who went away', as in McVeigh's book, but rather in terms of deities which have become irrelevant and, therefore, half-forgotten as Africans confront new historical circumstances. In northern Uganda, according to Okot, 'the Chiefdom deities perished during the first few years of colonial rule. Today there are many young men and women who know nothing about them.' Hence Okot's suggestion that the Christian God is conceived as just another deity by some Africans.

Mbiti's reply to this criticism is also very significant. In an open speech prepared for the visitors' Programme during the WCC Fifth Assembly, Mbiti answered this criticism by explaining that theologically speaking, he preferred to talk about *one* God not *many* Gods. God represents the the ultimate reality for which every human being has groped, and there are, therefore neither many deities, nor particularized deities for particular ethnic communities. There may be varying concepts of the same God, but there are not many Gods.

In almost all parts of contemporary East Africa where Christianity has been established for a long time, the beliefs of African peoples about their deities and their traditional religious ideas have been influenced by Christian doctrines propagated through the missionaries and their converts. Depending on the extent of the penetration of Christianity into African religious beliefs, the African concepts of deities have been relatively modified, often unconsciously, even among the older men and women. Therefore, when researchers go out into the field to study traditional African beliefs, they cannot avoid collecting data which show either apparent similarities between African deities and the Christian Concept of God, or the remoteness of African deities contrasted with the Christian God—it all seems to depend largely on the teaching propagated through the missionary enterprise, and the African response to that teaching within the particular historical circumstances. It is interesting to note, for example that the fighters for freedom in Central Kenya believed that God was on their side, and used the exodus motif as a source of theological encouragement. The traditional concept of God was enriched with new ideas and beliefs, to enable the fighters to confront their particular historical situation.

The collection and interpretation of such data is influenced greatly by the assumptions and interests of the researcher such as those which Okot p'Bitek has raised. The problem of communication also affects the quality and accuracy of the data which are collected, and these in turn affect the conclusions. African scholars ought to take these factors into account when they rely on earlier research into the impact of Christianity on Traditional African Religion. Samuel Kibicho observes this point cautiously, in his argument that there is continuity of the traditional Agikuyu concept of *Ngai* into the contemporary Agikuyu concept of the Christian God.

Okot p'Bitek doubts whether African deities will survive the distortions which they have received from Christian missionaries, and from the contemporary ideas in science and philosophy in Europe and America: Such ideas have made many Europeans and North Americans sceptical of the claims of Christianity. In science, the great achievements made in technology have led many people to doubt the fundamental Biblical faith in the ultimate power of humankind to change its environment and redirect its own history. In philosophy, this scepticism may be exemplified by such writings as those of Bertrand Russell in his book *Why I Am Not a Christian*.[23] Russel, having declared that he did not believe in God, went on to show why he could not believe in Jesus either as the Son of God, or as one of the wisest persons that ever lived. Such ideas make Christianity seem irrational, or they reduce it to a set of principles which are so ordinary that with the loss of uniqueness Christianity loses credibility among the academically educated Africans who are exposed to these ideas. Okot suggests that African deities will not survive invasion by these ideas, which are widely spreading in contemporary Africa through the mass communication media and academic education.

> Will the African deities survive the revolutions in science and philosophy which have killed the Christian God? I doubt it. Christianity has declined (in Europe and North America) because the Christian God used to fill gaps in science, or to deal with life at the point at which things got beyond human expectation or control. This has now been dismissed as intellectual laziness or superstition. The Christian and moreover, the metaphysical statements about him, do not make sense to modern man.[24]

Okot's criticism against Christianity is clear here. However, it is important to note that while many Europeans and North Americans have become sceptical of Christianity, at the same time the Churches in those countries have not entirely closed down, and a few prophetic Christian theologians have continued to interpret the Christian Gospel in terms which are relevant to their historical contexts. Such theologians have often been unpopular because of their criticism of the irrelevancies in their Churches. Among such theologians may be mentioned Paul Van Buren, Harvey Cox, John A T Robinson, Jurgen Moltmann,[26] and others. 'The death of God' debate to which Okot p'Bitek alludes, is not the only theological debate in contemporary Europe and North America. Within recent decades there have been, among others, the Secular-City Debate, the Honest-to God Debate, the 'Theology of Liberation', Racism in Theology and Theology against Racism, and so on. Thus, there have been positive voices within the apparently collapsing Churches, and it does not appear to me that Christianity will be altogether abandoned in those two continents. It has not been wiped out in places where Christians are persecuted for their faith, and in western Europe and North America, the Churches are still in favourable relations with the influential sections of society, including the governments.

Together with Okot's conclusion that African deities will not survive, is the implication that Christianity may also not survive in Africa, since its God will become irrelevant with the success of science and philosophy. After all the Christian God is already dead, as far as he is concerned. Yet, at the same time, there are now African Christian apologists, trained Churchmen and women, some of whom are highly qualified theologians. These theologians, with the help of missionaries both dead and alive, are trying to articulate the systematic African Christianity in terms which are meaningful and relevant in contemporary Africa. They are doing this at a time when the Churches in Africa are continuing to expand in membership, at varying rates of growth. Such African Christian apologists in contemporary East Africa include John Mbiti, Charles Nyamiti, Aloysius Lugira, John Gatu, Henry Okullu, Eliewaha Mshana, and others.

The fact that at present there are many contemporary East African critics and apologists of Christianity, makes the study of their debate a very timely investigation. This study has been a preliminary contribution to this concern.

Church Leaders

African religious heritage is not a scriptural heritage.[27] The liturgy of traditional African worship is not written in books of common prayer, or in Missals. It is interesting to note that the majority of African Church leaders do not write down their sermons and, therefore, it has not been possible to accumulate collections of texts which might illustrate how African Christians view Christianity. For the purposes of this study, it has been possible to draw on the written contributions by Joe Kayo. It is not the purpose of this study to explain why African Church leaders have for a long time not recorded their interpretations of Christianity. But briefly, it may be suggested here that the fact that literacy is traditionally not a necessary requirement for African worship, may have contributed to the situation. Further, Church leaders are often too occupied with various responsibilities, to be able to set aside time for writing down their sermons. By the very fact of their commitment to ordination, they indicate their conviction that Christianity is *The Answer* to all the spiritual problems and challenges facing Africans. Their pastoral responsibilities are concerned with helping those in difficulties, to find peace, rest, comfort and hope in Jesus Christ.[28]

There are different emphases among Church leaders with regard to the significance of Church tradition, African heritage, and the scriptures. The Roman Catholic Church, for example, lays great emphasis on Church tradition, and the Pope, being regarded as the Spiritual Apostolic successor of Peter, provides a universal unity in the Church.[29] On the other extreme, some Protestant Churches believe in the 'Priesthood of all Believers.'[30] These shades of the understanding of the Christian ministry in no way overshadow the common basis of Christianity namely, the Faith in Jesus of Nazareth. Christianity is based on the recognition and acceptance of Jesus of Nazareth, as Christ. Anyone who does not elevate Jesus to this unique position cannot be a Christian.[31] African Church leaders have already committed themselves to this faith, and accepted the responsibility of propagating the faith.

Many academically educated Africans find themselves unable to accept the Christian faith as it has been presented. Some of the reasons have already been indicated, but it is of importance to add that the image of Christian living which the Church leaders portray to their parishioners, has a great impact on the youth of the parishes. Ngugi wa Thiong'o illustrated that impact in his novel *The River Between*, when he presented a profile of Joshua, a Church leader who had nothing original in his thoughts and actions since he had become a Christian. He had become a 'parrot' of the missionary who lived at the mission station, and whenever a challenge confronted him with regard to the relevance of his faith in each context, the best he could do was to quote what the missionaries had taught him. Many academically educated East Africans consider Christianity to be a hindrance to creativity, because their experience has been full of African Christian leaders who abandoned their creative engagements in traditional life to join the routine of prefabricated Christian living.

The Church leaders in contemporary and future East Africa are increasingly and urgently confronted with the challenge of demonstrating that Christian living ought to be creative and constructive. So far the image of the African priest or pastor perceived by educated East Africans, has been passive and in most cases negative. The Church leaders have been seen as people who, after abandoning the traditions of African ancestors, have engaged themselves in a profession of prohibitions. The Church leaders in general have far too long been concerned with telling people what they *shalt not do*. The challenge now is for Church leaders to indicate what people should do in accordance with the Gospel.[32]

At another level, the uniqueness of Jesus Christ is not fully accepted by critics of contemporary East African Christianity. Taban Lo Liyong has emphasized that the presence of many Church traditions and conflicting political and economic interests, make it difficult for Christianity to witness effectively and positively in East Africa. Christianity, especially in Uganda, has portrayed more disunity than unity, in spite of the scriptural teaching that unity is necessary. The Ecumenical Movement, and the co-operation of the Roman Catholic Church with it may contribute to diminishing this impression, but it will take a long time, depending on the future witness of ecumenical endeavours. At the national level, the National Councils of Churches may contribute to the portrayal of the positive witness of Christianity. This has already begun happening in Kenya, where some of the critics of East African Christianity, such as Micere Mugo and Kabiru Kinyanjui, have recognized some positive trends within the National Christian Council of Kenya.

Church leaders will have to acknowledge the fact that Christianity is only one of the several religions in contemporary East Africa, some of which, like Christianity, claim to have universal appeal to all human kind.[33] Islam is one of the greatest challengers of Christianity in East Africa. Both Christianity and Islam are religions introduced from outside which continue to vie for an African following. Both have had an impact on African religion and the result of this interaction are not yet easy to describe with precision. Obviously, there will be advocates of each of these three religious traditions, and followers of each will be influenced to varying extents, by the other faiths. The World Council of Churches now recognizes the importance of taking the believers of other faiths seriously, and hopefully, this will change the attitude of some member Churches to the people who choose not to be Christians.

Among some academically educated East Africans, Jesus is considered as having no relevance in contemporary contexts, because he was a Jew who lived at a particular time in history and responded to the challenges of his time and place in his own way.[34] The teachings of other religious leaders of the world should also be given serious consideration, and Jesus should not be the criterion of individual and social conduct. Such people who hold this view, of course do not accept the divinity of Jesus. Christians ought to listen to these critics, because it appears that the acceptance or rejection of Christianity by someone always depends on his understanding of the Christian faith implied in practical living.

Something may also be said about the Churches as social institutions. They have structures that have been developed for a long time according to different traditions, so that the main Church denominations have within their administrative structure and their liturgy features that can be traced to the cultural roots of those denominations. At the same time, the Church as a social institution has certain relationships with other social institutions in a particular society. Very often in history, the Church has tended to support and provide theological justification for the existing structures, within other institutions. This, the Church leaders have done to ensure the mutual survival of the Church and State. The question arises as to what role the Church ought to play when other institutions are unjust. If the Church supports or justifies such structures, then it will lose its prophetic witness. This seems to have happened during the colonial period. For clarity, a distinction ought to be made between the moral and the legal notions of justice. The Church views justice from the moral perspective, whereas the State maintains the legal perspective. Ideally, the two perspectives should concur. In practice, however, the moral perspective serves as the foundation for law and law reform.

Other Interpretations

This general critique is cognizant of the fact that the bulk of this study is far from exhaustive. Someone else conducting this study might have selected other categories and people for discussion. It is taken for granted also, that there may be differences in interpreting one person's views of Christianity. For example, it is not expected that every reader will agree with the interpretation and criticism of Ngugi wa Thiong'o, Okot p'Bitek, John Mbiti, or any of those whose views are discussed here. Nevertheless, this study points to an approach of discussing Christianity in contemporary and future East Africa, which may be very rewarding.

During the initial stages of this study, it become clear that no list of categories would adequately cover the wide spectrum of interpretations of Christianity in contemporary East Africa. The present categorization was chosen for convenience. However, some educated people who have contributed to the discussion that is the concern of this study could not be fitted into the categories of creative writers, scholars, Church leaders and foreign missionaries. This section will not attempt to give a comprehensive survey of 'other interpretations,' because such an endeavour would be impossible to accomplish. However, a few of such interpretations may be offered a critique here, so as to illustrate what this apparently vague categorization implies.

Some political leaders throughout their careers have expressed their views about Christianity as it was introduced and propagated in East Africa. Some of them have been committed Christians within the 'established' Churches. Others, however, have contributed to the establishment of Independent Churches. Though it is unnecessary to list names of such politicians in this text, the contribution of these leaders in the interpretation of Christianity in contemporary East Africa, is of great significance.

The category of Church leaders has not been adequately representative. A whole volume could be written on the contemporary interpretations of Christianity by Church leaders. Thus, there are leaders of so-called 'established Churches,' leaders of Independent Churches, leaders of the recently introduced Pentecostalist Churches, and leaders of such a Church as the Deliverance Church, which claims to belong to none of these categories. There are lay leaders and ordained leaders, and this study does not make this differentiation. Then, there are those who are not Christians, but belong to other faiths. Some, such as Taban Lo Liyong, do not care about religion at all. In the preparation of this study, this great variety was taken account of, but preference was given to noting this wide variety within the category of other interpretations.

Artists also have expressed their views about Christianity, and Christian art is growing in contemporary East frica. Elimo Njau, Director of Paa Ya Paa and Kibo Art Galleries is one of the contemporary educated East Africans who has expressed his interpretation of Christianity. His murals at Murang'a Cathedral portray Jesus and his ministry in an African context. His paintings are a protest against the missionary presentation of Jesus as a white man, while Satan was presented as a black man. Such imagery, Njau has always argued, has the effect of making Africans hate themselves, and associate themselves with evil and with Hell. If Jesus proclaims a universal Gospel, and if the Kingdom of God is for all humanity, then Christ is as much European as he is African. Jesus was a Jew. But Christ, speaks to all cultures with the same challenging message.

NOTES

1. Bethuel A Ogot, 'A Man More Sinned Against than Sinning—The African Writer's View of Himself ' in Pio Zirimu and Andrew Gurr (eds.), *Black Aesthetics: Papers From a Colloquim Held at the University of Nairobi, June 1971,* Nairobi: East African Literature Bureau, 1973, p. 22.

2. John V Taylor, *Primal Vision,* London: SCM, 1963, p. 12.

3. ibid. p. 12.

4. Ali A Mazrui, 'Aesthetic Dualism and Creative Literature in East Africa' in Pio Zirimu and Andrew Gurr, (eds.) *op. cit.* p. 32.

5. B A Ogot, *op. cit.* p. 30.

6. Shorter, *The African Contribution to World Church and Other Essays,* Kampala: Gaba Publications.

7. See, for example, Hal Olsen, *African Myths About Christianity,* Kijabe, Kenya: Africa Inland Church Press, 1972, pp. 15-18, Kihumbu Thairu, *The African Civilization,* Nairobi: East African Literature Bureau, 1975, passim. S G Kibicho, 'The Continuity of the African Conception of God into and Through Christianity: With the Kikuyu conception of "Ngai" as a Case Study,' (Mimeo) Nairobi University, 1975. pp. pp. 4-11.

8. This assumption has been accepted and taken for granted by many African Christians. See, for example, Byang Kato, *Theological Pitfalls in Africa,* Kisumu; Evangel Publishing House, 1975, pp. 27-46.

9. Many European customs which missionaries brought with them were introduced to African converts with the explanation that they were Christian customs, e.g. marriage customs, feeding habits, dressing, etc. See Kihumbu Thairu, *op. cit.,* passim. Also, Okot p'Bitek, Africa's Cultural Revolutions pp. 1-5.

10. See, for example, *The Standard,* 24 July, 1975, p. 4.

11. Walter M Abbott, *The Documents of Vatican II,* London: Geoffrey Chapman Publishers, 1966, pp. 149-157.

12. Okot p'Bitek, *African Religions in Western Scholarship*, p. 116.
13. Interview with J S Mbiti. 6 Dec. 1975.
14. These questions constitute the body of McVeigh's book. In his opinion, the questions are answered affirmatively in Christianity, whereas in African religious heritage, the answers are either negative or vague. Hence his conclusion that only Christ can bring clarity and centrality to African religious thought. *op. cit.*, conclusion
15. Edwin Smith, (ed.) *African Ideas of God*, London: Second Revised edition (ed. E G Parrinder), 1961. Also E W Smith and A M Dale, *The Ila-Speaking Peoples of Northern Rhodesia*, Vol. I, London, 1920. The views of Smith are discussed in detail by Malcolm McVeigh, *op. cit.*, passim.
16. Okot p'Bitek, *African Religions in Western Scholarship*, p. 7.
17. ibid. pp. 108-109.
18. ibid. p. 109.
19. Kwame Nkrumah, *Consciencism: Philosophy and Ideology for Decoloniation*, London: Panaf Books, Paperback, 1970, pp. 97-98.
20. J K Agbeti, 'African Theology: What It Is' in *Presence*, Vol. V No. 3, 1972, Nairobi: World Student Christian Federation.
21. Okot p'Bitek, op. cit. p. 110.
22. ibid. pp. 110-111.
23. Bertrand Russell, *Why I Am Not a Christian*, London: Allen and Unwin, 1954.
24. Okot p'Bitek, *op. cit.* p. 112.
25. For a discussion of these theologians, see J Sperna Weiland, *New Ways in Theology*, Dublin: Gill and Macmillan, 1968 (Trans. from Dutch by N D Smith).
26. For example, Jurgen Moltmann, *The Crucified God*, London: SCM Press, 1973.
27. By this I mean its doctrines were not written, but passed on from generation to generation through oral transmission. This is in contrast to such religions as Christianity, Islam, Buddhism, which have books for basic reference.
28. I assume that the African Christians who offer themselves for ordination to priesthood are convinced that in Christianity lies the answer to all religious problems of humankind.
29. Walter Abbott *The Documents of Vatican II*, p. 344.
30. William Hordern, *A Layman's Guide to Protestant Theology*, New York: Macmillan, 1957, pp. 29-30.
31. All Christian denominations, Orthodox, Catholic, Anglican Protestant, etc. affirm Jesus Christ to be the head of the Church. See the Hymn 'The Church's One Foundation is Jesus Christ Her Lord', Redemption Songs, No. 50.
32. Jesus introduced a new approach of teaching in Judaism, by telling his followers what they ought to do, rather than what they 'shalt not do.' See 'Sermon on the Mount,' Matt. Chs. 5-7.
33. For example, Islam and the Bahai Faith, both of which have substantial following in East Africa. See *Kenya Churches Handbook*, Kisumu, Kenya: Evangel Press, 1973; F B Welbourn, *East African Christian*, Oxford University Press, 1965, pp. 54-62.
34. J G Donders has expressed his reflections on this point in a short sermon, see *Expatriate Jesus*, Nairobi: Gazelle Books, 1975, pp. 1-2.

Chapter Two

THE CHRISTIAN MISSIONARY ENTERPRISE

During the last quarter of the eighteenth century a new awareness arose among the Protestant denominations in Europe and North America. This led to the formation of missionary societies whose purpose was to spread the Gospel and Western civilization to the different parts of the world.[1] The nineteenth century was characterized in Europe by the Industrial Revolution, the transformation of political systems into modern nations, and the expansion of the political and economic influence of European nations outside the continent of Europe to Africa, Asia, South America and the Oceanic lands.

These features of nineteenth century Europe had a great impact on the Church—within both the Protestant and Roman Catholic Church contexts. The presuppositions underlying the Christian missionary enterprise of the nineteenth century, were nurtured under the impact of these features. In this chapter, some of those presuppositions will be examined. The missionary enterprise will be juxtaposed in the context of the events and ideas which were flourishing in western Europe throughout the nineteenth century, and whose effects continued into the twentieth century.

The relevance of this focus is that these presuppositions conditioned what the missionaries preached to the Africans, and that the teaching of the missionaries was received by the Africans positively or negatively, depending on the historical circumstances in which the missionaries confronted the Africans. It is not the primary concern of this book to discusss the *essence* of Christianity vis-a-vis the teaching of the missionaries.[2] Rather, the book highlights the response of Africans to what the missionaries called 'Christianity'. In nearly all the cases, Christianity was presented to the Africans as the religion and culture of Europeans, who at the same time thought of themselves as the perfect and highest model for the rest of humanity to copy. Though there were different emphases among the various missionary bodies who joined the enterprise of 'civilizing' and 'christianizing' Africa, yet their presuppositions were basically the same.[3]

Evolution

It is often quoted that the first two Protestant missionaries to East Africa in the modern period were Dr and Mrs J L Krapf, who arrived at Mombasa in 1844 as agents of the Church Missionary Society.[4] By 1844, 'evolutionism' in this context was understood to refer to the belief that both the animate and the inanimate, the organic and the inorganic aspects of this universe are in a continuing process of change, and that through this process, the various components of the universe are changing progressively from lower to higher quality.[5] Most Europeans, since the second half of the nineteenth century, believed that Europe had reached the highest peak of the evolutionary process and that the rest of the world was far below them in the ladder of evolution. Though the theory of evolution was expounded and popularized by Charles Darwin, (1809-1882) his followers and also his opposers, evolutionary thinking may be traced back to the eighteenth century.[6] Fichte and Schelling are reported to have held the idea that being is determined only by opposition and struggle against its opponent—a struggle ending in victory and subjugation. The difference between the positions held by Fichte (1762-1814) and Schelling (1775-1854) need not concern us in this study. However, it is important to note that the understanding of this universe in terms of the dialectical process was already current as early as the eighteenth century, and the views of Johann Fichte and Friedrich Schelling are illustrative cases.

The dialectical philosophy in which Nature was the absolute being that works itself out unconsciously, albeit purposively, as Fichte thought, was taken up by Friedrich Hegel (1770-1831). While accepting the dialectic interpretation of the Universe, Hegel rejected the assertion of Nature as the 'Absolute.' He asserted that the Spirit alone is 'Reality.' It is the inner being of the world, that which essentially is, and is *per se*; It assumes objective determinant form, and enters into relations with itself—it is externality (otherwise), and exists for itself, yet in this determination, and in its otherness, it is still one with itself—it is self-contained and self-complete, in itself and for itself at once.[7]

According to Hegel, Spirit was in the process of self-realization through the dialectic process, and history was a part of this unfolding. To Hegel, the Prussian Monarchy of his time was a 'grand climax' of world history, and there were other lower forms of political power structure. He thought that the first political form which we observe in history is Despotism, the second *Democracy* and *Aristocracy*, and the third *Monarchy*. This dialectical and evolutionary thinking was continued by Ludwig Feuerbach (1804-72), Karl Marx (1818-83), Darwin (1809-82), A R Wallace (1823-1913), Thomas Huxley (1825-95) and others.

While maintaining the dialectical interpretation, Feuerbach rejected Hegel's idea that ultimately the universe is 'Mind' or 'Spirit,' and instead, asserted again that nature is the ground of man.[8] He wanted to abolish the then predominant Christian idea of God as a spiritual and other-worldly being. In the place of this concept of God, he wanted to exalt nature to the level of the Christian God.

Charles Darwin and Karl Marx also accepted the dialectical and evolutionary interpretation, and tended to maintain the position that Feuerbach promoted. Darwin concentrated on illustrating the theory of evolution through biological observations. The publication of his book *Origin of Species* in 1859 caused a great stir among scientists and clergymen in western Europe, and heated debates followed, especially within the Church of England.[9] The objection to the theory of evolution was that it rejected the doctrine of creation, and if creation was rejected, the foundation of Christian faith would be shaken. The accepted Christian doctrine was that in the beginning God created the universe, and all things in it. According to Darwin, man as a species appeared on earth through a long process of natural selection, in which the living organisms changed in their internal and external structure so as to survive in their particular and changing environments. Man was therefore not, according to this theory, created by God and placed in the Garden of Eden as the Bible stated. Though Darwin expressed ignorance as to the origin of life, such agnosticism was not acceptable to the conservative Christians, who considered this view as anti-Christian scepticism.

Nevertheless, Evolutionism became steadily accepted, especially when the theory was extended to aspects of life and thought other than biology. Karl Marx, further expounded the position of Feuerbach and proposed the doctrine of historical materialism, which accepted dialectical interpretations of natural and social change.[10] He laid emphasis on history, and applied the dialectical interpretation of class conflicts in western Europe, particularly in Britain. According to him through the dialectical process manifested in class struggle and class conflict, society was continually changing and this change was progressing towards the ideal that would culminate in a classless and stateless society, that is in Communism. These ideas were systematized in the *Communist Manifesto*, which he launched with Friedrich Engels in 1888, four years after Dr Krapf had landed in Mombasa. Karl Marx exerted great effort to describe the stages he envisaged as necessary in the development towards the ideal, the communist society, that could be achieved through Dialectical Materialism.

By the end of the nineteenth century evolutionary thinking was widely accepted, and was extended beyond biology to other branches of knowledge, including religion, politics, history and psychology. In all these branches of knowledge, Europe was generally understood to have achieved the highest level of development, and there was a prevailing attitude of complacency, paternalism, and self-confidence. This attitude rapidly spread to the lower classes of west

European society, so that even those lower class missionaries who went to Asia and Africa considered themselves to have attained the highest possible level of civilization, which the 'primitive savages' were expected to copy in order to 'develop' from 'paganism' to 'civilization'. To indicate the wide acceptance of evolutionary thinking by the end of the nineteenth century, Owen Chadwick has noted that when in 1989 Fredrick Temple became Archbishop of Canterbury he had delivered Bampton lectures at Oxford twelve years earlier,[11] On the Relations Between Religion and Science.[12] These lectures assumed evolution as an axiom.

It was not, therefore, surprising that the elevation of Temple to the most senior Anglican office was bound to cause a protest. But the protest came from an unusual quarter. A clergyman by the name of Brownjohn had resigned his parish because he accepted evolution, a stand that was not acceptable for a clergyman of the Church of England. Brownjohn appeared at Temple's confirmation in Bow Church to lodge a protest against the faith of him who was nominated to be Archbishop. The Vicar-general overruled the protest.[13]

This trivial little incident, Chadwick suggests, may be taken to mark the final acceptance of the doctrine of evolution among the bishops, the clergy and the leading laity. Evolutionism became permissible and respectable in western Christendom.

Owen Chadwick also observes that for a decade or two after 1896, some members of the Church of England, especially among the evangelicals, most of the official members of the Roman Catholic Church, and most of the worshippers among the working classes, 'continued to know nothing of evolution or to refuse to accept it on religious grounds, that is, on their faith in the inspired truth of the Old Testament.'[14] This means that by 1920 there were still many lay Christians who were ignorant of the theory of evolution and the essence of its assertions. The first two decades of the twentieth century were decisive in the establishment of Christianity in East Africa, and it is clear that many of the missionaries who were involved in this enterprise, took evolutionism for granted even though they taught their prospective African Converts to accept only the doctrine of creation. Ironically, Africans who went to school learned the theory of evolution in biology, geography, chemistry and physics. Thus the teaching of missionaries concerning creation could not be reconciled with science lessons.

Social evolutionism is still widely presupposed, and it is used by many missionaries and technical advisers as a justification for their continued patronage over Africans, several decades after independence. The theory of biological evolution is still widely accepted, but the extension of evolutionism to social transformation is unwarranted by historical evidence. The universe may have evolved from simpler organisms to more complex structures. But there is no correspondence between this evolution in nature and the engineering of social structures through the coalescence and conflict of social interests, and the manoeuvres of influential individuals.[15]

There has been a violent reaction against social evolutionism among some of the *Asomi*[16] in East Africa, especially since the attainment of constitutional independence. Part of the criticism against Christianity arises from the belief which many missionaries have maintained, that Christianity is the highest religion for all mankind to follow, and that West European Christianity in particular is the highest form of expression which the rest of mankind must accept. On the other hand, other *Asomi* have apologized for Christianity, using the evolutionary presupposition as the basis for their argument. Such *Asomi* have followed the premises of their patron missionaries, and having accepted the West European or North American forms of Christianity, they have regarded themselves as having 'seen the light,' while those who are not yet Christian are described as 'still living in the darkness.'

Social evolutionism as a presupposition is one of the factors which determines the position held by the *Asomi* with regard to Christianity. Those who accept that Africans are 'primitive' while the Europeans are 'developed' and 'civilized,' also accept the Western expression of Christianity. They argue that the tradition of Christianity in that part of the world is long enough to have provided opportunities for the faith and practice to be tested. Therefore, it is argued, Africans should accept the Western form of Christianity as it has stood the test of time. Some of the apologists for Christianity who apparently reject evolutionism argue that if the missionaries came merely to introduce Christianity to Africa, then they have accomplished their mission and they should go back to their home countries so that the Church may grow to maturity and selfhood.

The Success of Science

The Industrial Revolution which spread throughout western Europe during the eighteenth and nineteenth centuries, led many Europeans to believe that their achievements in science had brought western Europe to the peak of human development. Although many Christians resisted the scientific theories which tended to undermine traditionally maintained Christian beliefs, even the most conservative Protestants and Catholics could not isolate themselves from sharing the material benefits of industrialization. The success of science in the second half of the nineteenth century led many people in western Europe and North America to believe that the evolution of society must be aided by industrialization. This belief was widely held by many missionaries and colonial administrators.

In North America, this belief was expressed and put in practice among the Black population, and the experiment of Booker T Washington at the Tuskegee

Institute, may be noted as an example. In that institute the freed Blacks were to be given basic technical skills which would help them to obtain gainful employment in the American economic system, which was rapidly becoming industrialized. The fact that the ideas of Booker T Washington were positively received by many influential people among the White population may be seen as an indication that industrialism was becoming a general presupposition in North America.[17]

Almost all the missionary societies who launched their work in Africa in the late nineteenth and early twentieth centuries, advocated the establishment of simple industrial centres in which African converts would be given technical skills as part of their recruitment into European civilization.

David Livingstone had earlier expressed his hope that the missionary enterprise would pave the way for commerce and Christianity in Africa. The products of industrialization, needed markets, and the factories needed raw materials. It is not surprising that several missionary societies in Kenya set up farms around their stations, in which they grew cash crops such as coffee. The coffee would be processed in Europe, and the African converts who worked on these farms would benefit only by being paid for their labour. The industrial centres set up by the missionaries were often planned to teach several skills, such as carpentry, masonry, and farming. But the skills were provided under the presupposition that if the so-called 'African Savages' were to 'be civilized,' they had to acquire the knowledge and skills which west European civilization had produced. To be a Christian meant to be 'civilized.' To be 'civilized' meant abandoning African life which was described as 'primitive' and 'savage,' and copying the west European way of life. This new way of life was characterized not only by a new moral code, but also by new technology, new norms in dressing, and new means of communication through writing and the railway. Industrialism was a presupposition which made the missionaries, colonial administrators, settlers and merchants look down upon Africans and Asians. The 'supremacy' of Europe was thus attributed to the success of science in that continent during the eighteenth and nineteenth centuries.

The success of science in western Europe had the effect of making most Europeans complacent and over-confident, because they thought they had achieved what other races could never achieve in the near future.

What was it that had given Europe its pre-eminence? Why had the Europeans alone, of all the peoples in all the world's history, succeeded in achieving universal domination?

The most obvious answer lay in Europe's technological superiority. Of all the great civilizations, only modern Europe had created a sustained dynamic and technical change. The Chinese—even the ancient Romans—were satisfied with a modest improvement of the technological achievements of their ancestors, but modern Europeans were driven to accelerate improvement, to speed growth from generation to generation in science and in techniques based on scientific method.

What are the implications of this presupposition for the responses of the *Asomi* to Christianity in contemporary East Africa? Many of the critics of Christianity have expressed disappointment because the Christian missionary agencies right from the beginning, allied themselves with the forces of imperialism, which justified the expansion of European empires by giving themselves the responsibility of 'civilizing' and 'Christianizing' the 'primitive races' of the earth. For example, Portugal, until the *coup d'état* of April 1974, continued to regard itself as a Christian empire, and justified its colonial domination of Africans by claiming that it was spreading and maintaining the Christian civilization. This claim was heavily criticized by Canon Burgess Carr, the then General Secretary of the All African Conference of Churches, who exposed an agreement signed in 1940 between the Pope and the Portuguese Government to co-operate in this enterprise of 'civilizing' and 'Christianizing' Africa through continued colonization.[18]

The critics of Christianity in contemporary East Africa have also challenged the presupposition that industrialization following the west European and North American patterns of economy and industry will necessarily solve the social, economic and political problems of Africa.[19] Some have pointed out that the Industrial Revolution led to the suppression and exploitation of the working classes by the industrialists and the merchants. The missionary enterprise which made such great contribution in influencing the Africans to accept the social, economic, political and religious values of Europeans, has since been criticized by many Africans, victims of this indoctrination.[20] A J Temu has observed that the mission policy found its chief critics in a majority of Africans who had passed through the missions.[21] Essentially, the missions taught and demanded submission and total obedience, neither of which could be reconciled with the rising nationalism of the Africans, led by mission graduates.[22]

The concept of development in which the west European and North American economic, political and industrial models are accepted as ideal for contemporary Africa is challenged by those who argue that the same people who had been oppressors during the colonial period would become neo-colonialists if they were allowed to advise on the models of development which Africans must follow after independence.[23] Involvement of Christian missionaries in the modernization of contemporary East Africa, has led some of the critics to revive the slogan which was common during the colonial period, that there is no difference between a missionary and any other European.[24]

Supremacy of Europe

The missionary enterprise cannot be fully explained without considering it in the context of European imperialism. The Berlin Conference ended with the partition of Africa between the powerful nations of Europe. The scramble for Africa which culminated in the partition, was a joint effort between the explorers, missionaries, merchants, adventurers and empire builders. For example, the presence of British missionaries in an area justified their claim of that area. Thus the presence of Dr Krapf and Rebmann at Rabai from 1846, and their 'discovery' of Mount Kilimanjaro and Mount Kenya in 1848 and 1849 respectively, justified Britain's claim to include Kenya in the British sphere of influence in East Africa. The Church Missionary Society had done very little in the interior of Kenya between 1844 and 1885, and yet, the mere presence of British sponsored missionaries in the area could constitute a claim to justify imperial expansion in that area.[25]

It has often been said that the involvement of Christian Missions in colonization followed several patterns, and that generalizations are unwise. This is true. In some areas, the missionaries preceded the colonial administrators. In other areas, they followed the soldiers who 'pacified' the 'natives' before the area could be 'open' to Europeans. Yet in other areas, the missionaries served as evangelists, administrators and civilizers, all in one. Nevertheless, it was generally true that the missionaries shared the excitement and ambitions of their respective home countries to dominate the rest of Europe, and if possible, the rest of the world. The Berlin Conference sought to settle the conflicts of interest between these powers, with particular reference to colonization.

During the First World War, many missionaries helped in recruiting Africans to fight, although the Africans did not know the causes of the war or the interests of those nations which were involved. The missionaries themselves knew that the defeat of their own nations would mean the suppression or termination of their enterprise in the regions where they operated with the protection of their governments. It followed, therefore, that they should participate in making their countries dominant powers in Europe, and in making Europe supreme over the rest of the world. In this connection, Roger Lloyd has suggested that one of the most significant events which led to the summoning of the international Missionary Conference at Edinburgh in 1910, was the defeat of Russia by Japan in 1905.[26] According to Lloyd,

> the missionaries saw more clearly than either the statesmen or the traders that this was a portent which completely changed the world situation and made all things new . . . . For many centuries before our own, the tide of human affairs had flowed westward and the historic

role of eastern and southern lands had been to serve the purposes of western nations. Only Japan had held aloof, successfully holding off all accidental exploitation . . . Her victory (at the Battle of Mouken) was complete and shattering at sea and on the land, and with this mighty portent, the twentieth century began. The balance of power between the nations was changed, the calculations of economists and financiers had to be redrawn, and the whole world situation was permanently altered.[27]

In Lloyd's view, here was a new challenge to the world, a new chance for Militant Christianity. Evidently Eastern nations too must soon assert their full equality with the Western nations of privilege, prestige and independence. The world knew it was becoming one entity, and people everywhere were dreaming of world empire. Would the principle of unity be the God of War or the Prince of Peace, Man or Christ? If this empire was to be claimed for Christ, the churches everywhere must co-operate in a gigantic effort. But it must be an informed effort; and to that end the first need was to gather, to pool, to co-ordinate all available expert knowledge of the new world situation. It was this first need which the promoters of 'Edinburgh 1910' set themselves to fill.[28]

Most missionaries thought of Europe as the stronghold of Christianity, and many believed that Europe had achieved greatness because its population and its governments had embraced Christianity. Thus, to defend and propagate 'European Supremacy' over Africa and Asia, would inevitably aid the missionary enterprise.

This belief also continued through the twentieth century, and was manifested in the missionaries who, almost all the time, sided with the administrators or with the settlers when the interests and welfare of colonized Africans were at stake. Although there were occasional disagreements between the three categories of Europeans (Missionaries, Administrators, Settlers and Merchants), the missionaries still thought of themselves as agents of Europeanization, and Africans thought of missionaries as part of the colonizing team.[29]

African critics of Christianity have often pointed out that during the Mau Mau emergency in Kenya, many missionaries were on the side of the colonial administration, that they abandoned the Africans at a time when the Africans really needed their help. Many of these missionaries were armed with rifles, and participated in the tortuous practices by which the colonial administration tried to wring information out of the Kenyans who were struggling for their independence.[30]

This observation has led many African *Asomi* to remark that the missionaries came to Africa with a Bible and no land, while the Africans had all the land and NO Bible. After colonization, the missionaries (and the other categories of Europeans) held control of all the land, while Africans were given the Bible to comfort them.[31]

It is interesting to note that Britain tried to present itself as the champion of the highest Christian ideal of love, by leading the campaigns for the abolition of the slave trade.[32] However, such a view would need to be challenged in the light of such views as that expressed by Eric Williams who argued that Britain's leadership in the campaign against slave-trade arose out of economic considerations, and not out of humanitarian or philanthropic benevolence.[33] The argument of Eric Williams may be convincing to an extent, especially considering that when the Clapham Group tried to move a bill through the British Parliament for the abolition of the slave-trade in 1789, the bill was defeated, and this led to the formation of the society for the abolition of the slave-trade. For Britain to change its policy radically in a matter of a decade, the considerations must have been other than the mere realization that slave-trade was against Christianity.[34] If the abolition of the slave-trade was inspired by Christian motives, it would have been unlikely for the colonial governments to oppress their subjects the way they did. Moreover, the slave trade would not have arisen in the first place!

The fact that the missionaries in their presumed superiority looked down and sometimes oppressed Africans in their schools, mission stations and churches, led to a contradiction which the 'mission graduates' observed, and which some of the *Asomi* in East Africa have exposed in their criticism of Christianity.[35] Jomo Kenyatta made his observations of this contradiction very clear in his book, *Facing Mount Kenya*.[36]

NOTES

1. S C Neill, *A History of Christian Missions*, Harmondsworth: Penguin Books, 1964, Part Two.
2. I have discussed various aspects of the essence of Christianity in my books *The Biblical Basis for Evangelization: Theological Reflections Based on an African Experience*, Nairobi: Oxford University Press, 1989; *African Christian Theology: An Introduction*, Nairobi: Heinemann, 1989; *African Heritage and Contemporary Christianity*, Nairobi: 1989.

3.   The problem of relating Christianity to culture has been explored in interesting detail by Lamin Sanneh, *Translating the Message: The Missionary Impact on Culture*, Maryknoll, New York: Orbis Books, 1989. See also H. Richard Niebuhr's two books *Christ and Culture*, New York: Harper and Row, 1951 and *Radical Monotheism and Western Culture*, New York: Harper and Row, 1943; Eugene Nida, *Customs and Cultures: Anthropology for Christian Missions*, New York: Harper and Brothers, 1954.

4.   A J Temu, *British Protestant Mission*, London: Longman, 1972, p. 5; Roland Oliver, *The Missionary Factor in East Africa*, London: Longman, 2nd ed., 1970, pp. 5-9; W B Anderson, *The Church in East Africa: 1840-1974*, Dodoma: Central Tanganyika Press. 1977.

5.   For a detailed explanation of the theory of evolution see, for example, George G Simpson, *The Meaning of Evolution*, revised ed., New Haven and London: Yale University Press, 1949.

6.   A lucid account of the debate over Charles Darwin's work is William Irvine, *Apes, Angels and Victorians: A Joint Biography of Darwin and Huxley*, London: Widenfeld and Nicolson, 1956.

7.   For a concise summary and commentary on Hegel's Idealism see Bertrand Russell, *History of Western Philosophy*, London: Allen and Unwin, 1941, pp. 701-715; Colin Brown, *Philosophy and the Christian Faith*, Downers Grove, Illinois: Inter Varsity Press, 1968, pp. 117-124.

8.   Ludwig Feuerbach, *The Essence of Christianity*, (1814), new edition, New York: Harper, 1957.

9.   The book *Origin of Species* went through many editions and reprints, the latest in Everyman's Library, 1959.

10. For a concise summary and commentary on Marx see Bertrand Russell, *History of Western Philosophy, op. cit.*, pp. 748-755; Colin Brown, *Philosophy and the Christian Faith, op. cit.* pp. 135-137.

11. Owen Chadwick, *The Victorian Church*, Part II, London: Adam and Charles Black, 1970, pp. 1-35.

12. ibid. p. 23

13. ibid. p. 23

14. ibid. pp. 23-25

15. A growing body of scholarship is challenging social evolutionism, and promoting other paradigms that are more realistic and representative. See for example, Chinua Achebe, Goran Hyden, Christopher Magadza and Achola Pala Okeyo, eds., *Beyond Hunger in Africa: Conventional Wisdom and African Vision*, Nairobi: Heinemann, 1990.

16. *Asomi* (literally, Readers). The term referred generally to those who had acquired the skills of literacy, that is, those who have gone to school. In this context it refers to those who might be loosely called 'academic,' or, *literati*. The term is used frequently in W B Anderson, *The Church in East Africa, op. cit.*

17. On this point see Kenneth James King, *Pan-Africanism and Education*, Oxford: Clarendon Press, 1971. This book is sub-titled 'A Study of Race Philanthropy and Education in the Southern States of America and East Africa.' Its focus is relevant for the argument of the present chapter.

18. Burgess Carr, 'The Engagement of Lusaka,' in *The Struggle Continues: Official Report of the Third Assembly of the All Africa Conference of Churches*, Nairobi: AACC, 1975, pp. 78-79. Lilyan Lagneau-Kesteloot, in *Intellectual Origins of the African Revolution*, (Washington DC: Black Orpheus Press, 1972, p. 86), reports that the agreement between the Vatican and Portugal was renewed periodically since the Papal Bull of Pope Nicholas V (1447-1455), which provided as follows:

> We, after scrupulous reflection, are granting by our Bull full and entire freedom to King Alphonso to conquer, to besiege, to fight, and to submit all the Saracens, Pagans, and other enemies of Christ, wherever they may be; and to seize the kingdoms, the dukedoms, the princedoms, the lordships, personal properties, landed properties, and the wealth they withhold and possess; and to submit these persons to perpetual slavery; to appropriate these kingdoms, duchies, principalities, countries, lordships, properties and wealth; to transmit them to their successors; to take advantage and make use of them personally and with their offspring. As they have received the so-called powers, King Alphonso and the Infanta have acquired, possess, and will possess, rightly and indefinitely, these islands, seas, and this wealth....

19. *Beyond Hunger, op. cit., passim.*
20. See, for example, Jo Ann White, ed., *African Views of the West*, New York: Julian Messner, 1972. This book contains excerpts from several African writers.
21. A J Temu, *British Protestant Missions, op. cit.*, pp. 9-10.
23. See, for example, Cees J. Hamelink, *Cultural Autonomy in Global Communications*, New York and London: Longman, 1983, *passim.*
24. Carl Roseberg and John Nottingham, *The Myth of Mau Mau*, Nairobi: East African Publishing House, 1966, p. 14.
25. The Missionary 'Scramble' for Africa is documented lucidly by Roland Oliver, *The Missionary Factor in East Africa, op. cit.* For the impact of the Scramble and Partition of Africa on the post-colonial quest for unity in the continent, see V B Thompson, *Africa and Unity: The Evolution of Pan-Africanism*, London: Longman, 1969.
26. Roger Lloyd, *The Church of England: 1900-1965*, London: SCM Press, 1966, pp. 195-200.
27. *op. cit.* p. 196-197.
28. ibid.
29. See, for example, S C Neill, *A History of Christian Mission*, Penguin Books, 1964, chapters 10 and 12.
30. Kamuyu wa Kang'ethe, 'The Suppression of African Patriotism and Nationalism by the Mission Churches in Kenya from 1900-1950,' in Ogbu Kalu ed. *African Church Historiography: An Ecumenical Perspective*, Bern, Switzerland: Evangelische Arbeitstelle Oekumene Schweiz, 1988, pp. 157-179.
31. *op. cit.*, pp. 161-162.
32. Philip Mason, *Christianity and Race*, London: Lutterworth Press, 1956, pp. 21-92.
33. Eric Williams, *Capitalism and Slavery*, London: Andre Deutsch, 1964. See also, Garth Lean, *God's Politician: Wilberforce's Struggle*, London: Darton, Longman and Todd, 1980; Folarin Shyllon, *Black People in Britain*, London: Oxford University Press, 1977.

34.   Eric Williams, *op. cit.*, pp. 145-153; Garth Lean, *op. cit.*, passim; F Shyllon, *op. cit.*, pp. 228-239.

35.   The mistreatment of Africans by missionaries at mission stations has been documented by A J Temu, *British Protestant Missions, op. cit.*

36.   Jomo Kenyatta, *Facing Mount Kenya,* London: Secker and Warburg, 1938.

Chapter Three

MISSIONARY VIEWS
OF AFRICAN CHRISTIANITY

The alliance between the imperial and the missionary factors in education amounted to much more than an alignment of theoretical policies. In terms of finance, the annual contribution of the British Colonial governments to mission scholars rose during the period between 1923 and 1949 from nothing to $285,000 in Tanganyika, from $10,000 to about $400,000 in Uganda, and from $14,000 to about $300,000 in Kenya. By the end of this period grants to missions were absorbing between half and two thirds of the educational budgets of the territories, and the individual missions were receiving more money from the colonial governments in respect of their educational work than their combined receipts from their home societies and from their local (African) church members. In some denominations more than a third of the European missionaries were supported out of government grants, while an even higher proportion received some official allowance in respect of part-time educational work[1].

Preliminary Remark

Roland Oliver, in his book the *Missionary Factor in East Africa* (1952) sketched the history of Christian Missions in East Africa. In his introduction to the 1970 edition, he pointed out his feeling that much of what he had written more than a decade before was still valid and useful as was demonstrated by the continued demand for his book.[2] A J Temu has added another scholarly study to Oliver's contribution, by publishing his history of the *Protestant Missions in East Africa.*[3] Several studies have been made regarding the historical setting of the Christian Missionary enterprise in East Africa, and there is no necessity to summarize them here.[4]

However, it is clear that the responses and interpretations that scholars in East Africa have made with regard to Christianity in the contemporary period, have been shaped by the historical setting of the missionary enterprise which introduced Christianity in East Africa. Before embarking on a detailed study of these responses and interpretations, it is helpful to examine the setting that has shaped their experience of Christianity. In his introduction to the 1970 edition of the *Missionary Factor in East Africa*, Roland Oliver wrote about the failure of the Churches, ever since the 1920s, to attract into the Christian Ministry even a handful of the best educated East Africans. During the first three decades of the colonial period, this had not been so. Of the first literate generation of East Africans the elite had become either chiefs or churchmen. But with the widening of secular opportunities, the churches began to be outpaced in the competition for the best educated men. With the introduction of higher education, the situation grew still more serious.[5]

Why did this situation arise? The churches and their agencies controlled education to a very large extent, although they received massive support from the imperial government. Although Oliver has documented the alignment of the imperial power and the missionary agencies, he does not seem to consider this alliance as a major factor that has contributed to the lack of commitment on the part of East African scholars, to Christianity as it was introduced to them. Rather, he implies, as seen from the quotation above, that the churches came into competition with secular opportunities and the latter won the services of the best educated men.

One of the prominent interpretations of Christianity in contemporary East Africa is that it was an instrument for furthering and justifying European colonialism and imperialism.[6] This interpretation is held by both Christians and non-Christians in East Africa. Hence, the opposition or indifference to Christianity among non-Christian East Africans,[7] and the advocacy of Moratorium and Indegenization of the Church by East African Christians.[8] Ngugi wa Thiong'o has described the missionaries as 'the colonial spiritual police.'[9] The fact documented by Roland Oliver that most of the missionaries were paid by the imperial government, gives a clue as to why such contemporary East Africans as Ngugi wa Thiong'o and the others discussed in this study, became critical of the brand of Christianity they received.

Welbourn's analysis of the Buganda community illustrates the role which the missionary societies played in breaking up the traditional ethnic order, and grouping the people according to allegiances based on religious faiths.[10] According to Welbourn, Muslims were not only third-class Ganda. They did not have, as did their Christian fellow-tribesmen, missionaries who could provide them with schools. In consequence, while Christians have found their ways into white-collar occupations and responsible administrative and political appointments, Muslims found status in the New Buganda through trade, primarily as butchers and taxi-drivers.[11]

Welbourn's analysis continues to show that even among the Christians there were differences which came to be reflected in the political life of Uganda at the time of independence. Welbourn exposes the difference between Protestants and Catholics: Protestants did not obtain administrative influence in Buganda merely because Lugard had given them political power. The tendency of Protestant education was to train for leadership. Missionaries established and administered their schools in the pattern of English public schools. Moreover, it was by and large the Protestant chiefs who grasped first the benefits of sending their sons for education overseas. Protestants thus maintained the lead which they had originally obtained almost by accident.

In Uganda, this denominational complexity led to a situation in which there were four categories of Buganda—Muslims, Catholics, Protestants and those who still followed the traditional religious heritage. The first three categories continued to keep some aspects of their old life, but they also acquired a way of life which had been inculcated into them through the effort of the Missionaries on the part of Christians, and through trading contacts with the Arabs and the Swahili on the part of Muslim Baganda.[12]

At the time of Independence in Uganda, these four groups came into open confrontation within the political parties that fought for dominance. The two most popular were the Democratic Party and the Uganda Peoples' Congress. Having considered the historical background of the various forces that fought for influence among the Baganda, it is understandable that the Catholics and the Protestants were leading in influence. The consequence of this division along religious and denominational allegiances led to the situation which was described by Welbourn. At least as early as 1890, Welbourn writes: 'Catholics, Protestants and Muslims in Buganda had formed indigenous political institutions, this social pattern with all its consequences was repeated throughout Uganda. Although it may to some extent have misrepresented the facts, it was no accident that during the election campaign of 1962, the Democratic Party was known popularly as *Dini ya Papa* (Religion of the Pope) and the Uganda Peoples Congress United Protestants of Canterbury'.[13]

Denominational rivalry and competition was not restricted to Uganda. In Kenya it was also common. Since the demarcation of mission spheres of influence before 1910, each denomination tried to keep other denominations out of its sphere, and to increase its membership even if this meant undermining or mispresenting the other denominations. Roland Oliver has expressed concern that since 1920, the response of the educated East Africans to Christianity has tended to be negative, or indifferent. It may be worthwhile to examine this in the light of Welbourn's analysis.

All the Christian denominations, both Protestant and Catholic, claimed to be proclaiming the Word of God, according to the Scriptures bound in the Bible. Yet these Christian Missionaries preached about unity which in practice they were operating against. Between the Christian denominations there was no visible unity, and no demonstrated effort to work together towards unity. The exceptions may be the Alliance High School and St. Paul's United Theological College in Kenya.[14] However, the High School was practically taken over financially by the Kenya Government before it was punctured by denominational competition, jealousy and rivalry. St. Paul's United Theological College has never become a successful achievement of inter-denominational co-operation, in spite of the several decades through which the college has survived. Denominational self-interest prevents it from becoming a successful ecumenical experiment. This is the view of some students and ex-students of that college and also of local and expatriate faculty who have worked there.

At the same time while Church leaders and missionaries preached about unity within the Church and out of it, disunity was rampant in the same quarters. The churches and mission schools taught that all people were created in the image of God, and at the same time the Europeans considered themselves fuller human beings than the Africans.[15] These and several other contradictions led the Africans who went through the colonial and missionary education system to become critical not only of the missionary enterprise, but also of the Church which the missionaries had established. This contradiction between credal statements and the practical expression of faith, led many East Africans to question the validity of the brand of Christianity which the missionaries and their followers were propagating. The challenges to missionaries by East Africans were expressed very early and *Facing Mount Kenya* is one such challenge.[16] The personal autobiography of Bildad Kaggia, entitled *Roots of Freedom*, also contains a personal account of such challenges.[17]

F B Welbourn, like most missionaries of his time, is an evolutionist. He presents the African thought as pre-scientific and non-intellectual. He contrasts between the 'civilized' and 'scientific' Europeans, as distinct from the 'uncivilized' and pre-scientific' Africans: Pre-scientific man Welbourn suggests, knows himself as a conscious, feeling, willing, thinking person and interprets the whole universe in these terms. He does not do so by an intellectual process of interpretation. But he uses an unconscious process in which his own feelings and emotions are *projected* on to the outside world. Scientific man, on the other hand, tends to interpret the world in impersonal, mathematical terms. He introjects (unconsciously adopts the characteristics of others) this interpretation into his understanding of himself. In the extreme case, the world becomes so depersonalized that he is no longer able to believe in God. He tries to interpret even his own consciousness in terms of chemical reactions .... Modern Europe and America are really *post-scientific*. They are much more interested in technology, in getting things done, than in understanding how they work.

Having described Africans as pre-scientific in their traditional setting, Welbourn goes on to observe that Europe and America have gone full-circle in the evolutionary process, and there is now 'actually a return to pre-scientific ways of thinking. Astrology and modern spiritualism take the place once held by tribal diviners and the cult of the ancestors.'[19]

Some East Africans have rejected this evolutionary thinking, and recognized it as one of the arguments used by missionaries and other Europeans to justify their religious, political and economic domination over Africans. 'Civilization of primitive peoples' was one of the arguments used to justify colonialism. Evangelization and civilization were considered as inseparable by most missionaries who felt concerned to bring the 'heathen' Africans from darkness to light.[20]

Welbourn also describes African thought as 'the thought of children,' following Jean Piaget's studies in child development.[21] In Welbourn's view Africans in traditional life thought like children of the civilized, scientific Europe, who had been studied by Piaget. According to Welbourn, another way of approaching and understanding East Africa's tribal background is through Jean Piaget's study of child development. Children start with the greatest difficulty in distinguishing between what belongs to the inner, conscious self and what belongs to the outside world. They assume that dreams come in at the door to visit them. So, pre-scientific men, when they dream of a neighbour or of somebody who is dead, assume that, in their sleep, they have received a visit from that person. This is quite automatic and implies no attempt to explain the affair intellectually.[22]

This attempt to understand African religious thought as "child-like", has been discussed in some detail also by J V Taylor in his *Primal Vision.*[23] The title of his book has these evolutionary connotations, although in Chapter Two of the book he claims that this was not his intention.[24] Taylor and Welbourn are contemporary missionaries, both of whom worked in East Africa and wrote about their experiences there. Welbourn continues to add more details to his evolutionary thinking, by discussing the concept of God. As far as he is concerned, the Christian concept of God as He is understood in Western European theological tradition, is the highest concept in the evolutionary process of theological thought. Africans were far down in this process when the missionaries arrived and need to be grateful for having been taught to know the 'true' God, as the missionaries knew Him.[25] All this kind of teaching, which was common during the colonial period till after independence in East Africa, was part of the setting which influenced the contemporary East African interpretations of Christianity, which are the concern of this study.

In the last chapter of *East African Christian,* Welbourn discussed the future of Christianity in the context of the quest for *African Personality, Identity and Nationalism.*[26] He wrote the book at a time when African leaders were beginning to formulate their ideologies for national independence and development. Negritude, Consciencism, African Socialism, Nationalism—All these were concepts under discussion as more and more countries became independent. The discussion among East Africans has shifted since then from these concepts, and when they are raised they are recognized as monuments to mark historical highlights in the development of African social and political philosophy.[27]

Welbourn felt concerned about the future of Christianity at that time because, in his opinion, the missionaries had failed to portray themselves primarily as Christians. Instead, they had portrayed themselves to Africans in such a way that Africans could not tell the difference between the missionaries and other categories of Europeans in East Africa.[28] This observation was true and this study will examine it in depth, and analyse the views of several East Africans with regard to it.

It is worthwhile to note Welbourn's assessment of the Christian witness of his fellow missionaries. He summarized his assessment in these words:

> By and large, it has been the national, rather than the Christian, identity of Europeans which has been obvious to Africans. This is so even in the case of missionaries, who may be wholly unconscious of their national bias. Europeans have been, after all, the living witnesses of Christianity. Seen through them, it has appeared to Africans primarily as a supernatural coat of paint for a sense of national superiority and determination to dominate others.[29]

Welbourn also made an assessment of the task with which East African Christians should be concerned. In spite of these failures on the part of the missionaries, Welbourn suggested that African Christians should not fall into the mistake of throwing Christianity overboard as a European importation. He challenged East African Christians thus:

> The practical task of East African Christians is to discover how it is possible, at one and the same time, to be identified both as African and as Christian. In this discovery they will make their contribution to the life of the world.[30]

This challenge is the main objective of the quest for *African Christian Theology*, a quest that is taking different emphases in different contexts all over the African Continent.[31] In South Africa, the quest has been given the label of *Black Theology*, because oppression of the majority in that country is on the basis of legalized colour prejudice.[32] In East Africa, the debate about *Moratorium* and the efforts to indigenize the Church, are all efforts towards the fulfilment of this quest.[33] Welbourn's challenge cannot be taken effectively by East African Christians unless they recognize the view of non-Christians who are also committed to seeing a successful future for themselves and their posterity. Committed East African Christians will have to convince the non-Christians that their faith offers workable solutions to the problems which confront contemporary East Africa. Unless they do this, the warped image of Christianity which Welbourn has vividly described, will continue to irritate academically educated East Africans, to the detriment of the Christian Churches.

Welbourn's own suggestion with regard to this challenge, is that Christians should take their commitment to the Gospel as the basis of their action and reflection, and should regard their social-political stand as secondary. The Christian claim, according to Welbourn, is that men are first of all children of God who may happen to be English or Baganda. But he observed that the majority of Christians consider themselves to be first Englishmen or Baganda who the happen to be Christian. This, he considers to be wrong.[34] Nevertheless, it is inconceivable for any Christian to live or express his faith except in a particular social-political setting. The individual discovers himself first as the child of his parents, and as a member of his community even before he is taught about God. Religion helps him to develop his spiritual values and integrity, and to establish a metaphysical justification for his involvement in the conduct of his community.[35] It is not the concern of this chapter to discuss Welbourn's assertion in depth, but it is worthwhile to note that one of the contemporary East African criticisms against Christianity as it was introduced, is the emphasis on universalism which has overlooked the necessity for East African Christians to become actively and constructively involved in shaping the destiny of their people. The missionary preaching, presented a universal Christ who was not interested in the liberation of Africans from colonial domination and exploitation, led many Africans to be negative or passive in the struggle for independence.[36] Consequently, many East Africans have become negative or indifferent to Christianity.

Welbourn's position with regard to the universality of the Gospel and the particularity of its reception, interpretation and expression, is typical of many missionaries during the last few decades of the colonial era. John V Taylor, a missionary who worked in Uganda, wrote that Christ has been presented as the answer to the questions a white man would ask, the solution to the needs that the Western man would feel, the Saviour of the world of the European world-view, the object of adoration and the prayer of historic Christendom. But many Africans are asking, what would He be like? If He came into the world of African cosmology to redeem Man as Africans understand Him would He be recognizable to the rest of the Church Universal? And if Africa offered Him the praises and petitions of her total uninhibited humanity, would they be acceptable?[37]

Taylor discusses these questions at length, but leaves answers open. Since he published *The Primal Vision* in 1963, the answers to these questions have been negative as far as his missionary successors are concerned. The quest for African Christian Theology has been viewed with suspicion and derision by most European and American missionaries, apart from a few exceptions.[38] Aylward Shorter is one of the few missionaries who have called for an African Christian Theology.[39] Adrian Hastings also has called for a new look at Church doctrine and discipline in the context of the African cultural and religious background.[40]

George Wayland Carpenter, another missionary writing to Europeans who wanted to become 'Christian pioneers' of mission in Africa, cautioned them that Africa is watching them.

> Many Africans would like to believe what we have told them about God, and Jesus Christ, and the way of love and truth. But a faith that seems valid only sometimes and in some places is not enough. Africans are looking to us for the validity of the Christian faith in our lives and circumstances.[41]

Further, Carpenter declared that there is one Lord and one faith. The mission too is one and in the end we see that God's mission is not ours. Before we came on the scene he was there; after we are gone he will still be at work.[42]

Having discussed the interpretations of Christianity from the perspective of a missionary at the period just before independence in East Africa, we may now proceed to discuss the interpretations of a missionary after independence during the contemporary period.

Of what value Aylward Shorter asks, are the opinions of a European missionary? It is of course ridiculous to pretend that a European can identify with the African mentality, or even as some anthropologists used to pretend, to preserve a neutral position. Nevertheless, it is possible to be a 'marginal African,' to possess an attitude of mind which disposes one to be actively understanding and sympathetic to African culture and to the aspirations of African Christians. This is not a passive role at all.[43]

Aylward Shorter writes as a Catholic priest and an anthropologist. His concern is that Christianity should not only take deep roots in Africa, but that African Christianity should make a contribution to the universal Church.[44] He is very concerned about the training of catechists, because he recognizes the fact that the spreading of Christianity in East Africa was largely the effort of catechists. 'This view is a correction of earlier historiography of Christian missions in Africa, in which the establishment of Christianity was presented simply as the exclusive contribution of European and American missionaries. Shorter emphasizes that without the contribution of the catechists, the spreading of Christianity would have been very much slower. He therefore calls for an intensification of the training of catechists, to carry on the work of spreading the Gospel.[45]

In *Missionaries to Yourselves*, Shorter and his co-editor emphasize the need for new methods of catechetical instruction in order that the Africans involved in evangelization may be well equipped to cope with the pastoral needs of contemporary African society. Shorter makes the same emphasis in his book, *African Culture and the Christian Church*.[46] Shorter's concerns in his missionary contribution are summarized in the first chapter of their book:

> One of the purposes of the book is catechetical: to discover those values and life-situations in contemporary African societies which can form a basis and a framework for preaching and for developing an African Christianity, a Christianity relevant to Africans today. Another purpose is moral: to acquire a correct understanding of contemporary African beliefs and practices, and to apply to them the relevant principles of a developing moral theology. Hitherto, these beliefs and practices have often been imperfectly understood by moral theologians. Yet another purpose is concerned with liturgy and with the need for the social apostolate to consider ways of handling African cultural material and African social institutions in order to install a living Church in Africa. [47]

Shorter, though conscious of the fact that he can never be an African, is concerned that every missionary working in Africa should thoroughly understand the cultural heritage of the Africans among whom he works so that he can communicate relevantly and meaningfully.[48]

He is one of the advocates of African Christian Theology. Writing in 1972, Shorter observed that much had been written about the subject, but that discussion had always centred on the nature and method of African theology, and not on its content. He called for a further development, in which, content would be put into this concern. His latest publication (November 1975) is a contribution towards this development.[49]

There are many objections to African Christian Theology, coming from both Africans and foreigners. The objections are based largely on ignorance, or on a misunderstanding of what the advocates of African Christian Theology seek to do. Shorter sees one of the main objections as the contradiction which many people see between the development of a theological reflection which is limited to a particular place and time, and the maintaining of the Universal Church is maintained. For such opposers, the development of particular theologies is a threat to the Universal Church. For many people, Africans included, a theology which is African and which is at the same time making a contribution to World Church, is a contradiction in terms, although, in fact, African socialists and political philosophers have long discovered that it is only when Africa has a contribution to make at a world level that she can be deemed to have any identity or originality.[50]

The opposers of African Christian Theology, Shorter observes, argue that the Church cannot be fragmented the same way as the African political philosophers sought for African identity. The Church, being catholic, transcends every culture in which her doctrines are expressed. However, Shorter dismisses that argument by emphasizing that African Christians must not be robbed of the opportunity to contribute to the growth of the Universal Church. Though the opposers of African Christian Theology have expressed the fear of pluralism in the Church if the African contribution is allowed, Shorter argues that a Church which lacks the African contribution cannot be claimed to be universal. He therefore, rejects the idea of merely translating particular European theological formulations and reflections into African languages. According to Shorter, the Church needs the African contribution for her own theological health. The African contribution is not going to destroy or alter the universal tradition, but it may first of all be a corrective in several ways.[51]

Shorter goes on to argue that African Christian Theology, in its corrective contribution, may awaken themes in Universal Christianity which are dormant or latent. He does not enumerate themes. Secondly, Shorter argues, African Christian Theology may help to show that certain elements presented to Africa as essential in the universal tradition are in fact secondary and deriving from the particular Western cultural tradition. In addition to this corrective contribution, there should be a positive role for African Christian Theology. Shorter emphasizes that the World Church has to serve, and speak to, a world in which Africans and Blacks generally, have an increasing voice. Africa is a fact to be reckoned with and the Church cannot afford not to enlist the services of African theologians to speak to this world. The universality of Christian Theology, therefore, turns out to be a developing universality, keeping pace with a World in evolution. African Theology will help the Church to open up new avenues for exploration, to develop a new awareness, in short, to cease to be a 'White Church.'[52]

This position has arisen out of the recognition of the fact that Africans have to be taken seriously as human beings, and as Christians. Before independence the foreigners, both in the colonial service and in missionary work, looked down upon Africans to such an extent that Africans were believed to be incapable of doing anything to develop themselves and their culture. Owing to the reactions which Africans were forced to launch both in and out of the Church, a few missionaries have began to appreciate the value of African contribution in the contemporary world. Shorter's view would have shocked such a missionary as Placide Tempels, who, in his sympathy for Africans, believed that he must think and speak for them, because Africans in his view were incapable of thinking and speaking for themselves. It is interesting to compare and contrast the views of such missionaries as Tempels, and those of contemporary missionaries, such as Aylward Shorter and Adrian Hastings. Placide Tempels wrote:

> We do not claim *of course* that the Bantu are capable of formulating a philosophical (or theological) treatise, complete with an adequate vocabulary. It is our job (of missionaries) to proceed to such systematic development. It is we who will be able to tell them in precise terms, what their inmost concept of being is. They will recognize themselves in our words and will acquiesce, saying, 'You understand us: you know us completely: you "know" in the way we "know".'[53]

Tempels wrote in 1945. Much later, in 1959, George W. Carpenter wrote:

> If African racial inferiority has no basis in fact, political patterns based upon it can hardly be justified today. Christians, especially, should be sensitive to their falsity, for equality of human rights and opportunities is a basic principle of Christian faith. God is the creator and father of all mankind . . . . The Gospel of Jesus Christ is addressed to all mankind without distinction. In him there are not Greek and Jew, circumcised and uncircumcised, barbarian, Scythian, slave, free man, but Christ is all, and in all.[54]

From the colonial period to the contemporary period there has been a change among some of the progessive missionaries, with regard to their attitudes towards Africans and African heritage. However, Africans continue to be suspicious of the missionaries, because of the discriminatory experiences they have gone through.

Shorter, being aware of this situation, feels that it is necessary to install a living Church in Africa, but he recommends the use of African catechists in this project.[55] At the Pastoral Institute of Eastern Africa, Gaba, Uganda, Shorter has been engaged in the preparation of these agents. He himself is now content to take the position of a 'marginal African,' so that he may be able to direct the project.[56]

One of the important questions in this study, is whether there is evidence that the African suspicion of missionaries is diminishing. Are Africans convinced that foreign missionaries in contemporary East Africa are working in the interest of Africa?

Shorter has declared his position. But as a Catholic priest, how widely are his views with regard to African Christian Theology accepted and supported by fellow Catholic priests, both African and foreign? Among Protestant missionaries, there is even greater reluctance to accept African Christian Theology. Most of them argue that there is only one theology, and that is Christian Theology. They **do not continue to add that the Christian Theology to which they are committed,** has been developed by European and American theologians, reflecting particular historical and social political contexts. When African theologians try to reflect about the practical implications of the Gospel in their own particular context, they are accused of being racial, and of wanting to divide up the Church, as if the Church is not divided already.[57]

One of the criticisms levelled against the development of African Christian Theology, has been that such a development will only express dissatisfaction and protest. The articulation of Black Theology in North America by James Cone and other Black theologians, has been quoted as an example of what may happen in East Africa if African Christian Theology is allowed to develop.[58]

Aylward Shorter, though a missionary, has an answer to give to his fellow missionaries.

> Theology must be contemporary and must be derived from modern cultural life. Nevertheless, it would be a grave mistake to assume that ancient religious ideas are not highly resilient in the modern situation. These ideas are often the last things to be affected by change, and they belong to the basic cultural coding of the African individual.[59]

Another fear of African Christian Theology is that it may sink Christianity into syncretism. With regard to this fear, Shorter answers the opposers of this development arguing that there is much syncretism in African Christianity already, because when the missionaries first preached the Gospel they did not bother to assess how it was received by Africans. The missionaries assumed that their African followers applied the same categories as themselves.[60] With regard to the continuity and discontinuity of African religious ideas in contemporary African Christianity, Samuel Kibicho has made a study on *The Concept of God Among the Agikuyu of Central Kenya.* His conclusion is in agreement with Shorter's view, that there was continuity, and the Agikuyu who became Christians took with them into Christianity, their traditional concepts of *Ngai* which they found to be basically similar to the missionaries' concept, even though the latter also introduced new teachings such as the doctrines of the son of God and the Trinity.[61]

As an anthropologist, Shorter is very interested in the symbolic significance of African social customs. He raises questions as to how these symbols might be used for the development of African Christian Theology.[62] This is a different approach from that used by Malcolm McVeigh, another missionary, who sees the coming of Christianity to Africa as a radical break from the African cultural and religious past. Whereas McVeigh observes vagueness in the African concept of God, or a contradictory understanding of God among Africans, Shorter, from a much broader anthropological perspective, sees this apparent contradiction as typical of all religious experience. McVeigh has observed that the Christian concept of God is one which emphasises immanence, omnibenevolence, as well as omniscience, omnipresence, omnipotence, and so on. However, he has declared that according to his research, God in African understanding is both Good and Evil.[63] This, it seems to me, is a contradiction in terms, and it may be asked whether a being who is understood to be Good and Evil at the same time, can be worshipped as God. What would be the purpose of the worship of such being?

Shorter, unlike McVeigh, is not so apologetic of Christianity as it has been propagated in Africa through the Euro-American Missionary Enterprise. In his view, the apparently contradictory sense of the sacred is common to all mankind, and to all religions.

Man, Shorter argues, describes the sacred from both a negative and a positive point of view. It is at once utterly unlike his own experience, and at the same time it is the perfection of that experience.

The sacred is totally 'other.' It is set apart holy, hedged round with prohibitions and taboos. It inspires fear. On the other hand, the sacred is 'ideal.' It is complete purity, wholeness, integrity, cleanness, order. It attracts, and fascinates, it invites restless man to undertake a continual search for development and perfection and assures him that his search is worthwhile. It is the blessing, prosperity and fullness of life.[64]

The sense of the sacred is not specifically Christian, nor specifically African. The apparent contradition is to be found in both religious traditions. On this ground, Shorter recognizes the need for Universal Christianity to be enriched by African cultural values and symbols. In this conviction he has the backing of Pope Paul VI, who has talked of the possibility, even the necessity, of having 'African Christianity.'[65]

It is interesting and surprising that the discussion about African Christianity should stimulate such heated debates among missionaries and African Christians. For it has been very clear that the missionary enterprise was characterized not by unity but by bitter competitiveness and division among the missionary societies and consequently among the African Christians who were converted to Christianity in the process of this rivalry.[66] In attempting to understand and explain the causes of the rivalry, it became quite evident that disagreements were not simply doctrinal. In Uganda, for example, the rivalry and competition between Anglicans and Catholics in the early period was at the same time a rivalry between English priests and French priests who were committed to bring the ambitious plan of Cardinal Lavigerie to fruition.[67]

Those who are against the development of African Christianity, seem to expect Africans to become Christians in a cultural and social-political vacuum, which is inconceivable. Otherwise, they must be expecting African Christians to express their faith without the socio-political commitment which such faith demands. How can African Christians testify to their faith without addressing themselves practically to the challenges which face those among whom they testify?

Shorter's answer to this question is clear. Christians all over the world are called to articulate their faith in terms which are relevant and meaningful to their contemporary situations, and to address their practical commitment to the challenges facing the society in each respective place and time. Hence, though he does not state it explicitly, Shorter would more readily appreciate the reflections of Black theologians in South Africa than those who come to preach about Jesus, claiming him to be the Saviour of all humankind without addressing themselves to the burning social, political and religious challenges facing the converts.[68]

Though only very few missionaries would go as far as Shorter in the attempt to make Christianity in East Africa distinctly African while at the same time evidently universal, history has shown that circumstances will force the rest of the missionaries to appreciate the African contribution to the World Church.[69]

The rest of this study is devoted to an analysis of various interpretations which East Africans both within and out of the Church, have made on the brand of Christianity which the Euro-American missionary enterprise has planted in contemporary East Africa. Although the establishment of Christianity was largely the work of African catechists and evangelists, these agents tried very hard to be faithful messengers of the missionary based in the various mision stations. Their acceptance of Christianity was based mainly on what the missionaries taught them, rather than what the Scripture states. Their interpretations of the scriptures remained faithful to the interpretations of the missionaries, and it was this faithfulness to the Missionary, rather than to the Gospel that led to the establishment of Independent Churches, especially in Kenya.[70]

NOTES

1.   Roland Oliver, *The Missionary Factor in East Africa*, London: Longman, 1952, New Impression 1970, p. 227.
2.   ibid, Introduction p. xi.
3.   A J Temu, *Protestant Missions in East Africa*, Nairobi: Longman 1973. See also his dissertation 'The British Protestant Missions on the Kenya Coast and Highlands,' University of Alberta, 1967. For a fuller Bibliography of Temu's works, see *Kenya Churches Handbook*, p. 328.
4.   A summary is provided in *Kenya Churches Handbook*, pp. 317-330. This is mainly for Kenya. More information can be found in *Occasional Research Papers*, Makerere University, in continual publications by the Department of Religious Studies.
5.   Roland Oliver, *op. cit.* Introduction pp. x-xi.
6.   For more discussion on this point see Judith Mbula 'Penetration of Christianity in Ukambani,' M A Thesis, University of Nairobi, 1974. Also, Erasto Muga, *African Response to Western Christian Religion*, Nairobi: East African Literature Bureau, 1975.
7.   They have reasons to hold this view, based on the collaboration which they noticed during the Colonial period. See F B Welbourn, *East African Christian*, Nairobi, Oxford University Press, 1965 pp. 64-69. Also Roland Oliver, *Missionary Factor in East Africa* pp. 231-292.
8.   For a discussion on Moratorium, see Burgess Carr, 'The Moratorium: The Search for Self Reliance and Authenticity,' *AACC Bulletin*, May-June 1974, pp. 36-44.
9.   Ngugi wa Thiong'o, *Homecoming*, London: Heinemann, 1972, Author's Note p. xvii.
10.   F B Welbourn, *op. cit* pp. 195-298.
11.   F B Welbourn, *Religion and Politics in Uganda*, p. 8.
12.   *op. cit.* pp. 9-10.
13.   *op. cit.* p. 1.
14.   The Alliance of Missionary Societies did not go beyond denominationalism.
15.   *East African Christian*, pp. 192-95.
16.   J. Kenyatta, *Facing Mount Kenya*, London: Secker and Warburg, 1983., *passim*.
17.   Bildad Kaggia, *Roots of Freedom*, Nairobi: EAPH, 1975.
18.   F B Welbourn, *East African Christianity*, pp. 31-32.
19.   ibid.
20.   Okot p'Bitek, *African Religions in Western Scholarship*, Nairobi: East African Literature Bureau, 1970, pp. 52-68.
21.   For a introduction to Piaget's works, See Ruth M Beard, *An Outline of Piaget's Developmental Psychology*, London: Routledge and Kegan Paul, 1969.
22.   F B Welbourn, *op. cit.* p. 32.
23.   J V Taylor, *Primal Vision*, London: SCM Press, 1963, pp. 42-47.
24.   *op. cit.* pp. 18-25.
25.   F B Welbourn. *op. cit.*, p. 42.
26.   *op. cit.* pp. 191-202.
27.   Taban Lo Liyong, *Thirteen Offensives Against Our Enemies*, Nairobi: East African Literature Bureau, 1973, pp. 78-104.
28.   F B Welbourn, *East African Christian*, p. 192.

29.   ibid. p. 193.
30.   ibid. p. 202.
31.   For brief surveys of efforts to articulate African Christian Theology, see E W Fashole-Luke, 'The Quest for African Christian Theology,' Paper presented at the Ibadan Conference of West African Association of Theological Institutions, September, 1974 (mimeo). Also, John S Mbiti, 'The Quest for African Theology.' Paper presented at the WCC 5th Assembly Visitor's Programme, Nairobi 1 December, 1975.
32.   For a discussion of Black Theology in South Africa, see Basil Moore (ed.), *Black Theology: The South African Voice*, London: Christopher Hirst and Company 1973.
33.   John Gatu, General Secretary of the Presbyterian Church of East Africa, was the first advocate of Moratorium in the current debate. The motto for his Church is *Jitegemea*, (Kiswahili) meaning Self-Reliance. A response to Gatu's proposal has been made by Henry Okullu, see *Church and Politics in East Africa*, Nairobi: Uzima Press, 1974, pp. 56-60.
34.   F B Welbourn, *op. cit.*, pp. 192-93.
35.   *Religion and Politics in Uganda*, pp. 62-63.
36.   Jesus taught within a particular community, with reference to a particular social-religious context. The Christian Gospel fails to be relevant if it does not encounter the challenges of a particular social situation. The Biblical Message cannot therefore be implemented uniformly in different parts of the world, since each country has its own social and historical background.
37.   J V Taylor, *Primal Vision*, London: SCM Press, 1963, p. 16.
38.   See, for example, the response of the elders and deacons of the Nairobi Baptist Church to the preparatory documents of the WCC 5th Assembly on the Theme— Jesus Christ Frees and Unites. See especially pp. 6-14 of the response.
39.   Aylward Shorter, *African Christian Theology*, London: Geoffrey Chapman Publishers, 1975. A review of this book was published in *Sunday Nation*, 28 December, 1975, p. 22.
40.   One of his main concerns has been the situation of Christian Marriage in Contemporary Africa. See Adrian Hastings, *Christian Marriage in Africa: A Report Commissioned by the Archbishops of Cape Town, Central Africa, Tanzania and Uganda*, London: SPCK 1973.
41.   George Wayland Carpenter, *The Way in Africa*, London: Edinburgh House Press, 1960, pp. 114-115.
42.   ibid., p. 115.
43.   Aylward Shorter, *The African Contribution to World Church and Other Essays*, Kampala: Gaba Publications, 1972, pp. 5-6.
44.   ibid, pp. 3-4.
45.   Aylward Shorter and Kataza (ed.), *Missionaries to Yourselves*, London: Geoffrey Chapman Publishers, 1972, Introduction.
46.   Shorter. *African Culture and the Christian Church*, London: Geoffrey Chapman Publishers, 1973, p. 2.
47.   ibid.
48.   Shorter, *The African Contribution to World Church*, pp. 5-6.
49.   See note 46.
50.   Shorter, *The African Contribution to World Church*, p. 3.

51. ibid.
52. ibid. p. 4.
53. Placide Temples, *Bantu Philosophy*, Paris, Presence Africaine, 1959. (Translated by Collin King), p. 36.
54. George W Carpenter, *The Way in Africa*, London: Edinburgh House Press, 1960, p. 59.
55. A Shorter and Kataza, *Missionaries Yourselves*. Also, *The African Contribution to World Church*, p. 9.
56. See notes 50 and 55 above.
57. The Ecumenical Movement has been striving for Church Unity, but its efforts have a long way to go before the ideal is realised.
58. Elders and Deacons of Nairobi Church, *Jesus Christ Frees and Unites: A Response to the Preparatory Documents of the WCC 5th Assembly* 1975, pp. 6-15.
59. Shorter, *The African Contribution to World Church*, p. 4.
60. ibid.
61. Samuel Kibicho, 'The Continuity of the African Conception of God Into and Through Christianity: With the Kikuyu Conception of "Ngai" as a Case Study'. Nairobi, 14 January, 1975.
62. This seems to be his main concern in *African Culture and the Christian Church* and in *The African Contribution to World Church*. For example, he has discussed African Feast and the Christian Eucharist, Notions of Sin in Traditional Africa, Christian and African Marriage.
63. Malcolm McVeigh, *God in Africa: Conceptions of God in African Traditional Religion and Christianity*, Cape Cod, Mass: Claude Stark, 1974, *passim*.
64. Shorter *African Culture and the Christian Church*, p. 46.
65. Shorter *African Culture and the Christian Church*, p. 1.
66. For a study of the history of Christian Missions in Kenya, see A J Temu, 'The British Protestant Missions on the Kenya Coast and Highlands,' Dissertation, University of Alberta, 1971. Also Mude Dae Mude, 'The Church and Traditional Africa, Commentary, *The Standard,* 10 January, 1976, p. 4.
67. Gideon S Were and Derek Wilson, *East Africa Through a Thousand Years*: Ibadan: Evans Brothers, 1968 and 1972, 2nd Edition, p. 174.
68. Shorter has written: 'It would not be realistic to expect the contribution of African Theology to be anything other than pluriform. African National Cultures are each developing in their own way.' *The African Contribution to World Church*, p. 3.
69. If Christianity survives in East Africa, and it seems likely to survive, it will not be possible for the World Church to ignore its contributions. Already, the Ecumenical Movement and the Roman Catholic Church have indicated the necessity to take the African Church seriously.
70. For further discussion of this view, see Judith Mbula, 'The Penetration of Christianity in Ukambani,' M A Thesis, University of Nairobi, 1974.

Chapter Four

HENRY OKULLU

One of the great issues in East African on which there is . . . much confusion concerns the relationship which exists, or should exist between Church and State. Every time this issue crops up both politicians and Christians are quick to refer to Romans 13, 'every person must submit to the supreme authority'. Although this is a universal principle to guide us at all times, our situation is different from that of the first century when Christians were sometimes claiming to be above the state and not subject to its powers. Today rulers are likely to demand more than their fair share and Christians are apt to become too subservient—thus preventing a healthy and balance(d) relationship between Church and state.[1]

The concern of Henry Okullu in *Church and Politics* in East Africa,[2] is the relationship between Church and State as institutionalized structures, and between individual Christians and the political situation in which they live. His questions try to raise the controversial among Christians with regard to this relationship. Although Paul's Epistle to the Romans states that Christians should obey those in authority,[3] Okullu raises the question as to whether this advice applies even when the rulers are unjust, when they have become totalitarian, or when they have become ineffective in their leadership.[4]

In his attempt to explain why this question has become urgent in contemporary East Africa, Okullu observes that the missionaries who introduced Christianity assumed that there was nothing of value in African religious heritage, and so they tried to make their African converts to abandon and forget their cultural background, in order to acquire the new faith.[5] The basic presupposition in this missionary exercise was that Christianity was inseparable from Western Civilization and, therefore, an African's acceptance of Christianity would automatically mean the imitation of the missionary's norms of conduct and living, including dress, food, eating habits, work and leisure.[6] However, the missionaries themselves were products of their Western culture. Even for them, Evangelization and Civilization were complementary aspects of the missionary enterprise. Before he could be baptized, an African had first of all to prove his maturity in the faith by demonstrating that he had acquired an 'adequate' degree of Western civilization.[7]

Consequently, the Africans found it difficult to distinguish, in practice, the difference between a missionary, a colonial settler and a colonial administrator.[8] All were members of the same race, heirs to the same culture, and beneficiaries of the same religious heritage. And this heritage happened to be Christian. Owing to this apparent inseparability between the missionary enterprise and the process of colonization, Africans accepted Christianity only as a functional means to help them survive in the humiliation, exploitation and oppression of the colonial system. But they did not allow Christianity to penetrate deep into their personality.[9] They could not, even if they would have liked to, because their cultural base had been destroyed in the drills of indoctrination.

Okullu observes that this background of the missionary enterprise meant that at the time of *Uhuru* (independence), most African Christians had not taken Christianity into themselves to the extent of being radically changed by it.[10] African Churches at independence found themselves in a situation in which the nationalists regarded the Church as one of the agents which the colonial power had used to maintain the colonial *status quo*. The fact that the teaching of the missionaries generally advised Africans to keep off politics,[11] aggravated this distrust of the Church. How would the Church conduct itself and address itself to the new situation under the new circumstances? This is a question which African Church leaders have not fully resolved, and which Okullu tries to provide an, answer.

His first premise, in his attempt to provide a solution, is that any solutions at which Christians may arrive through Bible study, are determined by the way in which these Christians understand the meaning of the Bible as the Inspired Word of God.[12] With regard to the relationship between Church and State, and all other matters in which the Bible may be consulted for guidance, Okullu's premise is that the Bible does not contain a code of instructions and regulations for Christian conduct. Rather it contains general principles which may help the Christian to think out a solution in any particular challenge.

Okullu suggests that there is no blue-print pattern of behaviour of Church/State relationship anywhere, which could be transplanted and fitted into the present situation in East Africa. Reference has already been made to Romans 13, in which St Paul issues useful pointers and guidelines, but like all the Biblical faith, this is a principle and not a prescription for Christian behaviour in any particular place.[13]

In Okullu's opinion, the situation of the Church in contemporary East Africa is similar to that in which it was during the period of the Roman Emperor Constantine. This was the first Roman emperor to offer Christians political protection, and this protection was understood to mean 'freedom of worship.' Having realized that the doctrinal controversies within the Church were causing political unrest and instability within his empire, Constantine authorized that a council of bishops and priests meet at Nicea, so that they might resolve the Asian controversy. The Nicene Creed, which is one of the most widely used creeds in the Church, was one of the products of the Council. The resolutions of the Council of Nicea cooled the controversy and the threat to the stability of Constantine's empire was averted. Thus Constantine, more than any other emperor, managed to tame the Church, and made it serve his political interests by giving it freedom of worship.[14]

Having made this observation, Okullu goes on to note that in contemporary East Africa, this experience was repeated when President Amin of Uganda, a Muslim, brought together the warring factions in the Anglican Church of Uganda. He held several conferences with Church leaders for the purpose of bringing unity in the Church.[15] The first meeting was held on 26 November, 1977, and addressed the delegates who included bishops, the clergy and the lay people of the Church. It was Amin's interest that there should be unity in the Anglican Church.

According to Mbiti, Amin summoned the delegates to meet at government expense, at the International Conference Centre in Kampala, to iron out their differences and disputes which had been simmering for about six years. He assured them that he would not allow anybody else to use the Conference Centre until they found a solution to their problems. That was on Friday morning and on the following Saturday evening he gave them until Sunday afternoon at 4 p.m. to reach an agreement. The next morning, Sunday, they celebrated the Holy Eucharist, and then the bishops by themselves went into a session of their own. When they held a plenary session that afternoon, they announced that an agreement had been reached, reconciliation had been achieved, and as a demonstration of this, the bishops spontaneously confessed in public their sins of hatred and impatience.[16]

Okullu suggests that the Church should not be too comfortable with this kind of Church/State relationship. The Christians may risk neglecting their responsibility to be the conscience of the nation. In his assessment, he finds that this relationship is very comfortable, sometimes too comfortable to enable the Church to fulfil its responsibility. In his book, *Church and Politics in East Africa,* Okullu has suggested that the Church in East African and its Councils are . . . having a very comfortable, sometimes too comfortable a relationship with the State and tend, in some areas at least, to be a mere government department with the responsibility of offering prayers for the leaders. Tragically this means that the call for the Church to be 'the nation's conscience' has gone unheard.'[17]

This observation that the relationship between Church and State is cordial, is confirmed by Bishop Raphael Ndingi Mwana a' Nzeki, Catholic Bishop of the Diocese of Nakuru, Kenya. In his article on Church and State in

Kenya, contributed to the *Kenya Churches Handbook*, Ndingi expressed the opinion that the Church and the State are two distinct societies, each of which has distinct concerns in the nation. The meeting point between Church and State is that each 'is composed of men, man and his welfare are the central issues.' [18] According to Bishop Ndingi, the Church is primarily concerned with the spiritual welfare of man as entrusted and commissioned to her by Christ. The state by the will and agreement of its people expressed in an agreement form, is charged with the material welfare of man. Each of these two societies pursues objectives according to circumstances of time, place, means and ability, but the fundamentals are the same—the common good: the one the spiritual common good, and the other the material common good. [19]

Ndingi suggests that the relationship between Church and State should be that of co-operation, 'in accordance with the African traditionalal motto. *Harambee* (Let us pull together).'[20] Further, he seems to be satisfied with the existing relationship between the two Institutions in Kenya. This is the general impression which Bishop Ndingi's article gives to the reader.[21]

Okullu, on the other hand, is very uneasy about the cordial relationship between Church and State, and his understanding of the nature of the two differs from that of Ndingi. According to Okullu, 'much of the trouble between Church and State arises from the false view of each in their proper relations with one another.'[22] It is, therefore, necessary to examine the various ways in which the purposes and relationship between the two have been regarded.

Some people, according to Okullu believe that Church and State are 'mere sides of the same coin.' This view is described as Erastianism, and it was the one held by such reformers as Luther, Zwingli and Calvin. Secondly, some think that 'the Church is Supreme and . . . the State is in a subsidiary position.' This, according to Okullu's observation, was the view maintained by the Roman Catholic Church throughout the Middle Ages. [23] It seems to be the view held by Ndingi, because he considers that 'Church and State relationships in our country (Kenya), based on the principle of subsidiary, have to date steered on the right course. This is a remarkable achievement, and one which other states might well look on with envy.' Again, he has written in the same context. 'The higher Church should not do what the lower (State) should do'.[24]

The third view is that Church and State should be completely separate. According to Okullu's assessment, Okullu observes that the Church in contemporary East Africa 'hovers vaguely between this (fourth) and the Erastian position.' [25]

Further, Okullu suggests a fifth view, to which he subscribes:

It is important to note that the Church and State are essentially different in origin. The Church owes its origin to Christ. The State is a divine institution of God for human society all over the World. The Church and State are created for different purposes. The State is created to keep Law and Order in society. Without outward civil order, no society can exist at all. The Church, on the other hand, is instituted by God to bring the mind of God to bear upon total human life and to contribute to the building of value systems upon which a sound human society may be built.

The Church claims no temporal power over men but appeals to their hearts and conscience. It is given to the right to correct, admonish or censure. Therefore, it is no interference in politics for the Church to warn the State that unrighteousness on public matters will bring calamity to the people.[26]

Having pointed out the dangers of too close a co-operation between Church and State, Okullu expresses his belief that 'There is both a strong theological foundation and a desire for a friendly relationship between Church and State'. He believes that it is the responsibility of the two institutions to 'work together in the task of building healthy and viable societies and in the moral and material development of our people.' While both Okullu and Ndingi agree on the suggestion that Church and State should share responsibility for social development, the two differ in that Okullu regards the two institutions as having been instituted by God for different functions, while Ndingi considers the Church to have a higher function than the State. In Okullu's view, both Church and State must recognize each other, as 'independent and distinct bodies in their entire office and function.'

The state must recognize that the Church has a divine right from God to possess and to use all the rights of correction and admonition invested in it without threat or interference from the State. The Church has the right to expect from the State a protection, a legal recognition of its character and freedom which it derives from God. The Church, on the other hand, recognizes that administration of public affairs belongs to the state. The formation of legislation and the enforcement of the same in so far as these do not contradict the will of God, are the responsibility of government.[27]

In order that the Church may be able to carry out its function as Okullu understands it, it is necessary to strengthen the ecumenical movement. National Church Councils, the All African Conference of Churches, and such other ecumenical bodies have an important role in enabling the voice of the Church to be heard by the State.[28] Okullu warns, however, that the National Council of Churches is likely to be 'looked at by government officials as a Super Church and matters of a national nature tend to be reffered to such a body.' For this reason, he stresses the need for the Churches to select able executive officers who should receive full guidance and support from the member churches.[29]

In all these aspects of contemporary East African life, Okullu finds that something has gone drastically wrong, with regard to development, he laments that the concept of development upon which nation-building is being conducted, is one which emphasises the accumulation of material possessions, such as permanent houses, better water supply, tarmac roads, better agricultural methods and products, more schools to educate more children, more dispensaries and hospitals to treat more patients, more nurses and doctors, permanent church buildings, better and faster means of communication—telephones, trains, buses, cars, aeroplanes, and such things.[30] Okullu notices that although some of the missionary societies tried to provide some of these facilities, they did not call it development. For them, this was part of the *service* they wanted to render in response to the command of Jesus that his disciples should go out and serve. He is concerned that many Christians have got trapped into the prevalent concept of development, with its overemphasis on material welfare. This, he warns, is wrong. He gives the following reason for disagreeing with this materialistic view of development:

> To the Christian, the development is not (ought not to be) just an accumulation of wealth but its fair distribution as well; not only the concern for economic well-being but also a real concern for the development of the whole man so that he can remain in control of the world he helps to create.[31]

Instead of man becoming master of creation, he has become 'overcome by greed for wealth and although he goes on and succeeds in acquiring wealth, his character, his integrity and his very soul can become mortgaged for wealth.' Okullu suggests that there should be a new concept of development, which emphasises improvement of the *quality* of life, and not the *quantity* of goods. Neighbourliness and concern for others, should become the basis of the new concept of development which he proposes.[32]

In his understanding of Christianity, economic and political justice and development are inseparable. He gets his insight from the account of Abel and Cain, from the teaching of the prophets, and from the parable of the 'Good Samaritan.' Implicitly, he criticises those Christians and Churches which have restricted their service only to those who are members of their denominations or fellowship. Christian concern, in Okullu's understanding, 'is with men (people) everywhere, no matter what their religion, their economic conditions, or their ethnic origin.'[33]

He expresses concern that most leaders seem to realize that love for men shows itself in justice—justice towards all. This in his view, is love in the Christian sense. According to Okullu, anything short of justice is not love but a mere slogan.[34] Corruption and tribalism are Africa's two chief devils which are preventing people from achieving qualitative development.[35] Corruption has been accelerated by the desire of people to get rich quickly, and by the deterioration of moral and spiritual values in contemporary African society: Okullu suggests four ways by which Christians should attempt to minimize the spread of corruption.

First, he suggests that there should be a Christian campaign, using literature, radio, television, preaching and teaching. He proposes this because, in his experience, 'no sporadic raids by some clergyman from the pulpit or half-hearted denunciation by a political leader will have any effect on corruption.'[36]

Secondly, he suggests that every Christian must contribute by refusing to corrupt or be corrupted by any one, and to avoid participating in corruption. A campaign which would not be backed and followed up with committed individual action would not succeed in eradicating corruption. He is aware that individuals in some circumstances may be victimized for such actions, but in answer to this, he says Christians who want to follow their Christian profession in every way will not escape suffering. A Christian should count it a joy to suffer on account of refusing to do evil, according to the manner of his master, Jesus Christ. Indeed, suffering is part of a Christian calling.[37]

Okullu's third proposal is that corruption should be fought through exposure. He admits that this is the most difficult way because it is difficult to prove, and it may lead to the loss of one's job, or to some other form of victimization. In answer to this, he uses a similar answer to that provided in his second proposal, adding that every upright step involves personal or even family, difficulties.[38]

The fourth proposal, is that the Church itself must fight corruption through prophetic preaching. He is aware however, that the Church cannot do this effectively unless it is also free from corruption. He draws his illustrative lesson from such prophets as Amos, Hosea and Micah who as individuals, accepted God's challenge to condemn corruption and other forms of injustice among the Hebrews of their time.[39]

Owing to the divisions which prevent Africans from thinking of themselves in national terms, Okullu suggests that the Churches would be more effective in combating corruption nationally, because the Churches often have broader bases among the members of the national community, than individual political leaders of trade unions.[40]

One of the most dreadful forces of division in contemporary Africa is tribalism. Okullu calls it Africa's second devil. In his opinion, the East African Revival Movement was the only movement in East Africa during the colonial period which managed to penetrate deeply beyond tribal barriers. However, he laments that the movement failed to raise the prophetic voice against tribalism at a time when such guidance was most badly needed. According to Okullu, this failure came from independence. When independence came, the militant used to bring political independence was now chanelled into the task of nation-building. This affected the Brethren of the Revival as well, many of whom saw and seized upon the opportunity to better their economic position, with the result that the (spiritual) militancy of the Brethren also died out.[41]

Okullu thinks that the Revival Movement in its strongest period was the peak of Christianity in East Africa, but in his opinion, the movement has deteriorated and become affected by tribalism. If the Revival is seen to have been the peak of Christianity in East Africa, then its members have recently clearly shown that their faith is no longer above loyalty.[42]

Okullu thinks that 'tribal affiliation has become the first consideration even among Christians.' On account of this, he attributes the failure of the Church union movement in Kenya, to tribalism.[43] Church union is commendable, in Okullu's view, because it enables the Church to speak with one voice in matters of Church-State relationship, and also in an attempt to fulfil the commandment of the Founder, that his followers may strive to become one. However, in his analysis of the failure of Church union talks, he suggests that *denominationalism* in the Church is 'another kind of tribalism, which keeps the smaller Churches away lest they become swallowed up by the big ones and make the bigger Church(es) arrogant and indifferent.'[44]

According to Okullu, tribal grouping as such is not bad, because it can be a great asset in nation-building. The strong family ties carried over from the traditional African community, can be used 'as a moral restraining influence upon, and a means of security for, its members.' This sense of oneness can be enlarged and modified to strengthen national identity. However, Okullu expresses concern over the fact that instead of 'tribal identity' being used for such positive ends, some ethnic communities have come to regard themselves as superior to, and better than, others. He suggests that no one ethnic group has got any justifiable reason to claim dominance over others, because those that appear to be powerful or influential acquire such status through geographical location, such as being in the highlands where the climate is cool and hard work throughout the day is possible, or through natural advantages, such as having fertile soil, and good rains which facilitates good agricultural yields.[45]

Okullu cites a book by Philip Mason, *Patterns of Dominance,* in which it is suggested that throughout the history of civilization, groups have acquired dominance, often by accident, and then have proceeded to make that accident a symptom of the universal process which intends them dominance. The process may be racial, tribal, religious, economic, cultural—but the product is the same—a group of people ruling by divine right, justifying their superiority, perpetuating their power by military or judicial instruments and demanding gratitude from the whole class which they rule.[46]

Examples of this can be cited in the case of the Portuguese colonies in Africa where religion—Christianity—was being used by the Portuguese to justify their colonial domination and exploitation over and against Africans.[47] Another example can be noted in South Africa, where a minority group of people originally from Europe, uses the Old Testament to justify the attitude of racial superiority and *apartheid*, separate development of races, in order to oppress, humiliate and exploit Africans.[48] Christians have a challenge to live beyond tribalism, and it is lamented, Okullu observes, that they have often failed to face this challenge, and followed the main current of tribal prejudice.

William Ochieng suggests that tribalism is a 'disease' which was introduced by the colonial powers, by inventing myths and propaganda which they used to alienate African communities from one another. To Ochieng, tribal identity is a good thing, because it provides a foundation on which an individual may become authentically African in the contemporary period. However, tribalism continues to be a mutual respect between the individuals within a nation and sometimes, even across national borders.[19] E S Atieno Odhiambo has made a study which supports the view that prejudice between ethnic communities against each other was invented and accelerated by Europeans when they came to settle and rule in the colonies they had conquered. One of the Europeans he cites is Karen Blixen, who wrote the book *Out of Africa*.[50]

With regard to the indigenization of Christianity, Okullu's assessment is that Christianity in contemporary East Africa is still too foreign to be able to speak effectively to African governments. He supports the suggestion that Christianity should be made indigenous to East Africa, but continues to define what he means by the term 'indigenization of Christianity.' But he differs with John Mbiti, who maintains that Christianity is already indigenous in Africa. Making Christianity indigenous does not mean engaging in a cultural excavation to resuscitate the Africa of a hundred years before Christianity came. African culture is what we are today and tomorrow.[51]

The Church in contemporary East Africa must speak meaningfully to Africans in various situations and background—rural, urban, literate, illiterate, employed and unemployed, rich and poor—to all sectors of the East African society. Okullu sees Africa as being 'divided' into two—urban Africa and rural Africa.[52] For urban Africans, it is meaningless and unacceptable to insist that African traditions and customs which are considered backward and unhygienic, should be introduced into Church life. He gives the example of eating habits in which the urban Africans have already taken the Western habit of using knife and fork, not only because that habit is 'civilized,' but because it is hygienic. However

Okullu considers it absolutely necessary that Christianity should be enriched by those aspects of African heritage which are valuable, and which are lacking in the brand of Christianity which the missionaries brought to East Africa.[53] He is aware that it will be difficult to introduce such aspects into the contemporary established Church because, though its leaders are African, they are Africans who copied and accepted the norms and interpretations of the missionaries who introduced Christianity to these Africans. In spite of these difficulties which he foresees, Okullu suggests, that African theologians have great responsibility to express the Gospel in African terms. Okullu's definitions of African (Christian) Theology, is as follows:

> African theology is not an antidote for the missionaries' complete rejection of every indigenous religious concept. Rather, it is an honest, positive appraisal and re-assessment of the essentials of the Gospel. Rejecting the impression that the African religious background is one whole lot of superstitions, taboos and magic, the theologian's task is not, however, to Christianize what is African, but merely to express the Gospel in African terms. African theology does not aim to found a new Church for the Africans only. There can be no other foundation beyond that which is already laid: Jesus Christ Himself. (1 Cor. 3:11)[54]

Byang Kato supposes that 'African Theology, as proposed by African Christian theologians, such as John Mbiti, John Agbeti, Manas Buthelezi, and Henry Okullu, is an attempt to exalt the non-Christian religions, including traditional African ones to the level of Christianity.'[55] But, both Okullu and Mbiti do not think of African (Christian) Theology in this sense. Kato as an African Christian evangelical, following the presuppositions of some missionaries and his colleagues at Dalls Theologial Seminary, made a very negative assessment of his own African religious background. In his opinion, 'African religions' do not even merit to be called religions. They have not provided any solution to human spiritual problems.[56] In agreement with his American colleague, George Peters, he sums up his assessment of African religions and of African Theology in the following words:

> Clues which only highlight human dilemma, man's craving for the ultimate reality, and yet constant flight from Him through the worship of idols, is all that can be found (in these religions). There is emphatically no possibility of salvation through these religions. But subsequent studies will show how many theologians today are trying hard to elevate these non-Christian religions to the same status as Biblical Christianity. The proposed 'African Theology' gives that impression.[57]

Neither Mbiti, nor any of the other African Christian theologians try to do what Byang Kato has accused them of doing. Mbiti's conviction with regard to the relationship between African heritage and Christianity, is summed up as follows:

> A theology which deals with Christianity in Africa must take into consideration the African concept of time, the meaning of death, the relationship between the living and the dead and the far-reaching consequences of the African discovery of the third futuristic dimension of time.[58]

There is no doubt in Mbiti's writings that Christianity has a contribution to make to the African heritage. But Kato's concern is that most of the African Christian theologians have given greater credit to the African heritage than it deserves from a Christian.[59]

Henry Okullu, while accepting the basic Christian doctrine that Jesus Christ is the only foundation of the Church, accepts that even though this doctrine is not in dispute among Christians, the expression of the life of the Church must reflect the daily life and needs of the people among whom the Church is located.[60] Byang Kato fears that the Church may be diluted or polluted by syncretism if African heritage is taken seriously by African Christian theologians.[61] Okullu, who himself is a bishop of the Anglican Church, is aware of such a danger, but he does not consider that a good excuse for ignoring the importance of the African heritage for the development of Christianity in contemporary East Africa. Present Church leaders in East Africa will have to be convinced by the (Christian) theologian that Christianity is not being diluted by heathen beliefs and practices from which we have been salved. Fear of syncretism has been one of the main obstacles to indigenizing Christianity in East Africa. Most of the present Christian leadership is drawn from those who were taught by the missionaries, and who are determined to keep the Christian faith 'pure.'[62]

Byang Kato, in Okullu's analysis falls in this category of Church leadership. 'Missionaries have got no future' in East Africa, in Okullu's opinion. However Okullu does not accept wholly the proposal of some East African Church leaders, that the missionaries should go back home and withdraw their funds from Africa for some years, so that the Church may be able to exercise self-reliance and assess the impact of the missionary enterprise. This proposal for the suspension of missionary aid in funds and personnel, has commonly been referred to as a *Moratorium,* and it has been discussed very widely since the Bangkok Conference of the World Council of Churches in early 1973. John Gatu was the most prominent advocate of the Moratorium[63] to emerge from East Africa. He still is at the time of the present study.

Okullu's view with regard to the Moratorium, is that it is not really the solution to the problem of self-reliance in the Church. Rather, it is that the missionaries must change their attitude towards their work and towards Africans. The missionary must quickly put aside the old concept of coming to Africa to lead and guide the Church.[64]

According to him, the solution is for the missionaries to come on short contracts to do specific projects, after which contracts they should return. These projects should be drawn by Africans in the interest of the African Church.

He is critical of those fellow East African Church leaders who advocate the moratorium, and at the same time invite the political leaders to do fundraising and lay foundation stones for Church buildings. Such closeness between Church and State, in Okullu's opinion, may be more dangerous than the impact of the missionary enterprise on the Church in contemporay East Africa. The Church, while local in its expression, must retain its universal character, and a categorical rejection of international missions would deny the Church this universal dimension.[65]

Okullu also has something to say about crime and punishment. In his view, it is one of the roles of the Church to guide the society from going the 'wrong' way: It is the Christian's duty to be answerable to society at large as to what solutions Christianity has to offer with regard to such problems as the place of the individual in society, drug addiction, prostitution, relationship between the sexes, property, marriage, family life and many others.[66]

With regard to crime and punishment, Okullu suggests that a person who has broken the law should be regarded as 'something in need of treatment, rather than punishment.' This suggestion should be supported by Christians because Okullu argues, 'It expresses a high regard for human life.' He proposes that there should be detention centres rather than prisons, and that death as capital punishment should be abolished in favour of detention in such centres where the criminals would be taught and given a chance to reform. Though expensive, this suggestion should be accepted if the society is going to accord every individual member full human dignity.[67]

'The Christian's sympathy should lie more with the offender as, in our present situation, he is the man most likely to lose his right (as a citizen).'[68] This view of crime and punishment is close to one of the trends in contemporary Christian Theology all over the world which emphasises that Jesus identified himself with and was on the side of the oppressed. James Cone, a Black American Christian theologian who advocates this view, observes that in the North American situation, the most oppressed section of the society is the Black population, and in that context blackness has become a symbol of oppression.[69] Until the Civil Rights Movement rose against the system, legislation was established with a bias against the Blacks, so that crime and punishment tended to be aimed at keeping the Blacks quiet in subordination to the white population. Blackness, for James Cone and other American Black theologians, is a symbol of oppression, and when **he says that God is black, he is making a symbolic proposition, and not a** statement of empirical fact. American Black (Christian) Theology is a contextual Christian theology, just like Black Theology in South Africa; and the Theology of Liberation in South America; propounded by such theologians as Manas Buthelezi and Gustavo Gutierrez, respectively.[70]

Okullu's other reason for proposing a revision of the contemporary codes of crime and punishment, is his observation that very often the offenders are not the only ones entirely to blame for the offences they may commit. The social structures in which we live contribute to the character of the individual members of the society which is ordered through those structures. Therefore, no one individual can be held to be entirely responsible for the offence he may have created. So, Okullu concludes that the sooner we come to terms with the fact that the type of crimes prevailing in our society are a by-product of the kind of societies **we are building, the better. It is true that creativity and hard work flourish best in an atmosphere of competitiveness but it is true that our present patterns of crime have something to do with living in a highly acquisitive society.** It is, therefore, more responsible and Christian to try to help John Juma than merely to condemn him to the role of the hangman.[71]

Okullu's general assessment of contemporary East Africa is that there is something seriously wrong with the trend of development. There is an over-emphasis on acquisition of material property, and a neglect of spiritual values. The following is his vision of the society East Africans should strive to build:

> A prosperous, strong and free society. A society in which many of the evils which we have been talking about (corruption, tribalism, drug **addiction, prostitution, and so on) are minimized and subordinated to the** common good. A society in which individual men and women have full opportunity to realize their full human political and socio-economic potentials. A society in which each man can make the fullest possible contribution to the welfare of his brother. A society in which a few elite do not abrogate to themselves the right to prescribe to their fellow men the extent of the freedom the latter might possess.[72]

In his opinion, neither the acquisition of modern education, nor the building of strong economic empires, will succeed in bringing the East Africans to realize this vision of society. Examples from all over the world, have taught him that these two cannot fulfil humanity's total aspiration, unless something else is added to the struggle. In his opinion, something of fundamental importance is missing in the contemporary efforts of development. This must be recovered, in order to set these efforts on the right track again. The missing link is spiritual, not material.

So, what shall we do? Okullu asks. It is obvious that we must go right down to the root of the matter, which is the loss of our spiritual values. Our spiritual lives have become choked and clogged by the accumulated debris of life. 'As for what was sown among thorns, this is he who hears the word, but the care of the world and the delight in riches choke the word and it proves unfruitful' (Matthew 13:22). To build the kind of society we are talking about requires and demands the uncovering of the basic resources of God.[73].

In Okullu's view, the strong economic empires of the Western world, though they have become overburdened with materialism, were initially built on the foundation of the Christian Gospel, and so it is ridiculous for Africans to aspire to build such strong empires on the Western model, while at the same time rejecting the spiritual basis on which those models were based.[74] Though Western form of democracy is not ideal, in Okullu's view it is closer to Christian teaching than other ideologies in the contemporary world.[75] He values greatly the zeal of the missionaries who sought to bring the Christian message to Africa, and pleads with African Christians in contemporary East Africa to re-discover the spiritual roots which they have lost.

One important question which Okullu does not discuss, is how the Christian Church should conduct itself in contemporary East Africa, with regard to the other religions prevalent in the area. Islam and the African heritage are strong in the three East African states, and Christians cannot conduct themselves in a manner which ignores the existence of these other religious traditions. The contemporary constitutions of these countries are secular, and it may, therefore, be expected that religious persuasions other than Christianity, also deserve a comparable role and equal treatment before the law.

NOTES

1. Henry Okullu, *Church and Politics in East Africa,* Nairobi: Uzima Press, 1974, p.7.
2. Henry Okullu has also been a frequent correspondent in the daily newspapers in Kenya, on matters concerning the freedom of expression and criticism.

3.   Romans 13: 1-7.

4.   *Church and Politics in East Africa,* pp. 7-8.

5.   ibid. p.8.

6.   Roland Oliver, *Missionary Factor in East Africa,* London: Longman, 1952, Second Edition, New Impression, 1970, p.122.

7   See, for example, 'A Biography of Molonket Olokorinya Ole Sempele' in Kenneth J King, and A I Salim (ed.), *Kenya National Biographies,* Nairobi: East African Publishing House, 1971, p. 24.

8.   F B Welbourn, *East Africa Christian,* p. 64.

9.   Okullu, *op. cit.* p. 8.

10.   Okullu observes that Christianity has not become indigenous to East Africa and supports the effort of 'Indigenization.' John Mbiti maintains that Christianity is already indigenous in East Africa. See, Chapter 5 below.

11.   This teaching meant that Africans should not criticise or rise against colonialism and imperialism. They should acquiesce under the oppression, exploitation and humiliation of their masters. In this way, the missionaries generally collaborated with the colonial administrators and settlers.

12.   Okullu, *op. cit.* p. 11 Also J N K Mugambi, *The Biblical Basis for Evangelization. op. cit.* pp. 32ff.

13.   Okullu, *op. cit.* p .11.

14.   ibid. p. 12.

15.   ibid.

16.   John Mbiti, 'Church and State: A Neglected Element of Christianity in Contem porary Africa' in *East Africa Theological Journal,* No. 5, Dec. 1972, p. 31.

17.   Okullu, *op. cit.* p. 13.

18.   Rafael Ndingi, 'Church and State in Kenya,' in *Kenya Churches Handbook,* p. 43.

19.   ibid, p. 44.

20.   ibid, p. 44.

21.   See note 54 below.

22.   Okullu, *op. cit.* p. 15.

23.   ibid. *op. cit.* p. 15.

24.   Ndingi, *op. cit.* p. 46.

25.   Okullu, *op. cit.* p. 15.

26.   ibid. pp. 15-16.

27.   Okullu *op. cit.* p. 19.

28.   ibid, p. 20.

29.   These topics constitute the chapters of Okullu's *Church and Politics in East Africa.*

30.   Okullu, *op. cit.* p. 21.

31.   ibid, p. 21.

32.   ibid, pp. 23-24.

33.   ibid, p. 24.

34.   ibid. p. 25.

35.   ibid. pp. 25-35

36.   ibid, p. 40.

37.   ibid, p. 41.

38. ibid. p. 42.
39. ibid. p. 42.
40. ibid. p. 42.
41. ibid. pp. 43-44
42. ibid. p. 44.
43. ibid. p. 45. See also, F B Welbourn, *East African Christian*, pp. 12, 192.
44. Okullu, op. cit. p. 45.
45. ibid. p. 46.
46. ibid. p. 46.
47. This situation has radically changed with the independence of all Portuguese colonies in Africa.
48. For a more detailed theological criticism of apartheid, see Johannes Verkuyl, *Break Down the Walls: Christian Cry for Racial Justice.* pp. 21-42.
49. William R. Ochieng, an essay on Tribalism in *JOLISO* (Journal of Literature and Society), Vol. No. 1, 1972.
50. She was an early settler who wrote an autobiography with interesting details on the prevalent attitudes of Europeans on Africans from various ethnic communities.
51. Okullu, *op. cit.* p. 52.
52. ibid. pp. 52-53. See also Okot p'Bitek, *Africa's Cultural Revolution,* pp. 100-101.
53. Okullu, *op. cit.* p. 24.
54. ibid. p. 55.
55. Byang Kato, *Theological Pitfalls in Africa, passim.*
56. Kato, *op. cit.* p. 45.
57. ibid. p. 45.
58. J Mbiti, 'African Concept of time' in *Africa Theological Journal,* No. 1, February, 1968, p. 22.
59. Kato, *op. cit.* pp. 32-35.
60. Okullu, *op. cit.* 56.
61. Kato, *op. cit.* pp. 28-29.
62. Okullu, *op. cit.* p. 55
63. John Gatu, Address to N C C K Luncheon Forum, Nairobi, 8 January, 1976. He emphasised: 'The Debate of moratorium is not dead.'
64. Okullu, *op. cit.* p. 58.
65. ibid. p. 60.
66. ibid. p. 61.
67. ibid. p. 65.
68. ibid. p. 67.
69. James H. Cone, *Black Theology and Black Power,* New York: Seabury Press, 1970. See also Charles Long, 'Structural Similarities Between African and Black Theology' in J N K Mugambi and Kofi Appiah Kubi (eds.) 'African and Black Theology' in *Journal of Religious Thought,* Washington, DC: Howard University Press, Vol. 32 No. 2 (Fall-Winter, 1975).
70. J N K Mugambi and Kofi Appiah Kubi (eds.) *op. cit. passim.*
71. Okullu, *op. cit.* p. 68.
72. ibid. p. 77.
73. ibid. p. 80.
74. ibid. p. 79.
75. ibid. p. 71.

Chapter Five

JOHN S. MBITI

Through the missionaries' preaching and the European kind of Education, Africans are discovering the future dimension of time. On a secular plan, this leads to regional planning and economic development, **political independence, and educational facilities. In ecclesiastical life,** this discovery seems to result in a marked expectation of the millenium, so that many Christians evade the demands of this life and simply hope and wait for a life in paradise. This marked expectation of the millenium often seems to be accompanied by a messianic hope which leads, among other things, to the formation of small independent churches clustered around a leader who symbolizes and partly fulfils this hope.[1]

In his works, John Mbiti has been concerned with studying the relationship between Christianity and the African religious heritage. To make his studies deep and systematic, he has selected two main concepts and explored them as they are applied in Christian Theology, and in African traditional thought. The first of these concepts is Time.[2] Eschatology features prominently in Christian doctrine, and Mbiti has come to the conclusion that New Testament Eschatology differs radically from the African concept of the future, and this radical difference has led to the consequence that new forms of Christianity are being evolved by African Christians, based on their own traditional concepts of time.[3] The second concept is that of God. Mbiti in his studies has observed that there are many similarities betwen the African concept of God, and the Christian concept of God. Thus in Mbiti's *Concepts of God in Africa*, he has systematically arranged the observation that Africans generally think of God as being omnipotent, omnipresent, omniscient, immanent and transcendent. These are categories of thought which are described in Hellenistic terminology.[4] Okot p'Bitek, one of the leading critics of Mbiti in East Africa, accused Mbiti of being and 'intellectual smuggler,' of 'dressing African deities in Hellenic metaphysical husks which have been discarded by the Christian God.'[5]

In Mbiti's opinion, Christianity is indigenous to Africa.[6] This point of view has also been criticized by East African scholars and artists. Mbiti's argument in defence of this view is that although Christianity was established in Africa South of the Sahara only during and after the nineteenth century, Christianity was established in Northern Africa and in Ethiopia very much earlier. When the continent of Africa is considered as a geographical unit, Mbiti argues that his opinion is consistent with the facts. It is true, however, that as far as historical studies have shown so far, Christianity did not reach Africa South of the Sahara prior to the fifteenth century. Ethiopia is regarded as being part of North Eastern Africa in this statement. The early contact of Christianity with Africa South of Sahara was through the Portuguese explorers, although through them, Christianity did not take root. It is clear in Mbiti's works that when he concentrates his studies on the interaction between Christianity and African heritage, he is mainly dealing with Africa South of the Sahara, because Northern Africa is predominantly Islamic. But, is the argument that Christianity was established so early in Northern Africa sufficient reason to conclude that Christianity is indigenous to Africa South of the Sahara? It seems that owing to the radical difference in the history of these two sections of the African continent, in discussing the establishment of Christianity in Africa the two sections ought to be considered separately. Mbiti has taken this approach in one of his latest books, *An Introduction to African Religion*. However, his answer remains affirmative to this question.[7]

John Mbiti is a Christian scholar. He is a Canon of the Anglican Church. As a committed Christian, he is convinced not only that Christianity is indigenous to Africa, but also, that Christianity is necessary for the guidance of human development in Africa. In his view, Christianity is indigenous to Africa because it is a response to the Gospel, not an imitation of the conduct of missionaries. According to him, Christianity has all the tools and instruments for guiding personal morality and spirituality, in building character (honesty, truthfulness, hard work, responsibility, etc), in equipping people to meet the trials of life such as sexual immorality, family tensions, feeling of loneliness, especially in the cities, in caring, loving, and giving the feeling that the individual matters infinitely as a person, as a human being. The Christian faith is a deeply human affair: it puts the person at the centre; it loves him and transforms him.[8]

It is as a committed Anglican Christian that Mbiti conducts his scholarship, and writes down his findings. This is demonstrated by the fact that in all his published scholarly works, he devotes the whole or a part of each publication to Christianity. In a lecture he delivered to a conference organized by the Church of Uganda (Anglican) in 1970, Mbiti declared that Christianity is neither a visitor nor a tourist in Africa, and that Christians must be at the forefront of all change and development in Africa: Christian involvement should be shown at all the frontiers of national change and development. We cannot halt change, no it is necessary, but at least as Christians we can sit behind the steering wheel and direct change, influence change, and redeem change when it seems to lose the way. National development should be for the betterment of society and if so, then Christians ought to be at the very front lines, with the understanding that this is God's world and that God is transforming it through Jesus Christ. In other words, we desperately need a theology of development here in Africa where so much emphasis is rightly being put on development. Christian involvement is also demanded in the field of revolution: social, cultural, political, and above all spiritual revolution.[9]

While Mbiti holds Christianity in such high esteem, some other East African scholars do not regard it as highly. William Ochieng , for example, thinks of Christianity as a drawback to African development, and cannot recommend any African leader who is a Christian. In an exchange of views between himself and Canon Burgess Carr, Ochieng' declared that Canon Carr was not a 'true' son of Africa, because he was a Christian.

For William Ochieng , Christianity represents Europe's cultural imperialism in Africa. It is a contradiction for an African to be committed to the positive and constructive development of Africa, and at the same time claim to be a Christian. In his criticism of Burgess Carr, William Ochieng wrote that by believing in the myth of Christianity, people like Reverend Carr are not only destroying themselves, but they are also fighting against the natural creative ability of the African race . . . . They are helping to maintain and uphold Europe's cultural imperialism in Africa . . . .

Unless Reverend Carr proves to us that the ideals of African religions were against "salvation by God of all men, man's liberation from sin, man's liberation from various forms of oppression and exploitation, man's liberation from himself and his own human affections," it is contradictory of him (Carr) to support the liberation movements in Africa while at the same time he preaches the cultural values of the Europeans in Africa.[10]

Scholars like Ochieng have responded to Christianity as it was brought and established by missionaries from western Europe and America. This brand of Christianity in general tended to justify colonialism, on the ground that the Africans were living in spiritual, physical and intellectual darkness, and they needed "salvation" and "civilization" through the missionaries and the colonial administrators. In order to establish missionary work, the Christian missionaries needed the protection of their respective colonial administration. The Africans needed to be "pacified" and brought under colonial rule before the missionaries could do their work.[11] Though this sequence of events did not apply in some parts of Africa, the East African development of Christianity left many Africans, upon reflection, with the conclusion that "there is no difference between a Mission and European." (Gutiri Mubea na Muthungu).

Whatever their theological outlook, missionaries were, in fact, involved from the start, in many other activities apart from preaching of the Gospel. Roman Catholics believe intensely in the mission of the Church as the source of all true civilization. They see the 'mission of civilization' as a necessary part of preaching the Gospel. They, therefore, had no hesitation in establishing plantations, whose profits would support their converts. Presbyterians and Moravians further insisted on the importance of commerce. In order to protect ties which were economically self-supporting. They tried to implant in their members the spiritual value of skilled and honest labour of the hands. The Moravians further, insisted on the importance of commerce. In order to protect their converts from Indian and Waswahili merchants, they established their own trading stations. The Scottish mission at Kibwezi was founded by three directors of the Imperial British East Africa Company.[12]

Whatever theological motivations the missionaries may have had, they did create the impression that in practice, they were collaborators with the colonial administrators, settlers and merchants. It was this impression that made some of the African leaders begin to question the sincerity of the missionaries, and of Christianity as the right religion for Africans.

William Ochieng does not consider Christianity to be indigenous to Africa. As far as he is concerned, it is a means used by Europeans to perpetuate their cultural imperialism in Africa. Ochieng, therefore, disagrees with Mbiti though he has not made a direct attack on Mbiti's position.[13]

Another scholar who differs with Mbiti is Kuhumbu Thairu. In his book *The African Civilization*, Thairu has written that Christianity is foreign to the African and not a universal religion as the colonizers and others before them taught.[14]

Thairu's arguments are different from those of William Ochieng. To him, Christianity is foreign to the African not because it is European, but because it is Jewish. Jesus claimed to have come to the world to fulfil the Law of Judaism; to clarify and exemplify the teaching of the Hebrew prophets. His teaching was from the standpoint of the beliefs and practices maintained by his compatriots. Thus, the reception he received from his fellow Jews, was based on the historical, political and religious background of the Jews of his time. Thairu explains his argument in these words:

> For what reason is Christianity a foreign religion to the Africans? Christianity is a development from Judaism. The Christians actually claim (or at least they wrote that their founder claimed) that Christianity is the fulfilment of Judaism. Of course this, the Jews deny. To the Jew, Christianity is a splinter group started by the followers of one of their minor religious teachers (Rabbis). The strength of Christianity

> lies in the belief that the founder Joshua (Jesus in Greek) from Nazareth
> was the son of Jehovah (Yahveh). Who was this Yahveh? Yahveh is the
> Jewish version of what we Africans call Katonda, Mungu, Mulungu and
> many other names depending on the language.[15]

In Thairu's view, Christianity was *misused* first by the Romans for their own imperial expansion to build the so-called 'Holy Roman Empire,' and later by other Europeans for the establishment of colonialism and commerce. Thairu observes that the pattern of the life of Jesus from birth to resurrection was not new in the history of religions. The deity Osiris of Egypt had lived, died and resurrected on the third day, over one thousand years before Jesus. Other religious figures, such as Krishna in India also had similar, though not identical, biographies.[16] In conclusion Thairu has argued that it is, therefore, erroneous to believe that a splinter of the Jewish religion is the universal religion. After all Africa had seen 'Jesus' i.e., Osiris over one thousand years before the Jewish Jesus appeared. Besides the Jewish Jesus is a fulfilment of the messianic dreams according to Christians. The dreams arose out of the Jewish context to fulfil Jewish ambitions. I fail to see how the African can come to regard them as his own.[17]

Thairu differs with Mbiti further in the discussion about God. Okot p'Bitek also criticises Mbiti, but using a different argument.[18] Thairu argues that the Christian God was a Jewish deity, who was interested only in the welfare of this chosen race, the Hebrews. In the Old Testament, this deity authorized the Hebrews to exterminate the Canaanites, so that the Hebrews may settle in 'The Promised Land.' Though the Hebrews were never masters in the Middle East, they had a theology which always explained their historical and political plights. The doctrine of 'election' was complemented by the doctrine of the 'remnant,' so that even when the Jews were taken to Babylonian Exile, the prophets were reported to have prophesied that a faithful remnant would return to the city of God, Zion, Jerusalem, to await the establishment of God's Kingdom through a Messiah. Christians believed, and continue to believe, that Joshua of Nazareth, Jesus Christ, fulfilled that 'Messiance' hope, not for the Jews alone, but for all human kind.[19]

The Church became, in Christianity, the New Israel—the New Chosen People of God. But the New Israel could not be understood apart from the Old Israel, and the New concept of Yahveh who was believed by the Jews to be the author of Hebrew history. Chapter 1 of the Gospel of John tried to bridge the theological and philosophical chasm that existed between Hebrew theology and Greek philosophy. As far as Thairu is concerned, this is an exercise which should not have been attempted in the first instance, because it was unjustifiable on grounds that Hebrew religion and Greek philosophy (and religion) were two distinct traditions which needed no complementation. He explains his position in the following words:

> A people's idea about God is entirely personal, as in the case of the Jews, and in many cases, very prejudiced. The Hebrew God was, and is still, the preserver of the Hebrew people against the blows and buffets of their environment, be it human or physical. Where the interest of the Hebrews and these other races (including Africans) conflicted, the Hebrew God did not hesitate, he upheld his people as a good responsible God would. When Hebrews were defeated and subjugated, they interpreted this as either punishment for their evil or as a temporary trial of faithfulness which was to be followed by prosperity and a subjugation of the oppressor. In short the non-Hebrew could never win. The Hebrew would, always, with the help of his God, get his own way if not on this earth (Here and Now), at the Messianic Kingdom anyway.[20]

Mbiti on the other hand, has argued that Africans believe that God is omnipresent, omnipotent, omniscient, and all the other attributes to which Christian Theology accords the Christian God. Okot p'Bitek challenges this, by arguing that this kind of linguistic terminology does not exist in African religious thought and that African deities are not understood by Africans in such categories as omnipresence, omnipotence, omniscience and so on.[21] According to Okot p'Bitek, the African deities of the books (including Mbiti's *Concepts of God in Africa*, 1970) clothed with the attributes of the Christian (Hellenized) God, are, in the main, creations of the students of African religions. They are all beyond recognition to the ordinary Africans in the countryside.[22]

Okot's views have been discussed in greater detail in the preceding section. Mbiti further suggests that the African concept of 'Time' is the fundamental concept underlying all the religious and philosophical foundations of African peoples. His studies have led him to the conclusion that Africans do not conceive of the future. Africans should be thankful to the missionaries because they have led Africans to discover the future dimension of time. In Mbiti's view, Africans pay attention to a two-dimensional concept of Time, 'with a long past, a present, and virtually no future.' This conclusion has been dominant in most of Mbiti's works.[23] In one of these works, Mbiti expresses his findings in the following way:

> The linear concept of Time, with a Past, Present and Future, stretching from infinity to infinity, is foreign to African thinking, in which the dominant factor is a virtual absence of the Future.[24]

According to Mbiti, Christianity is indigenous to Africans, and with it has come the teaching about the future dimension of Time. He is convinced that the linear concept of Time is a concept which Africans should adopt from the teaching of the missionaries.[25] Africans in Mbiti's observation, are short-sighted in planning because in their traditional thinking, they do not conceive of the future. According to him, far sightedness in African planning is difficult to acquire because the long future dimension of Time is lacking in our (African) traditional concepts of Time. We *must* create this vision so that the decisions we (Africans) reach and the plans we make are not just near-sighted, but far-sighted both in terms of the local situation and in a global way, since the Gospel is a universal gift for all times and in all places.[26]

Africans conceive of a future which does not extend beyond a few seasons, according to Mbiti. This short future is actually part of the present, and constitutes what Mbiti calls *Potential Time*. Time is not real until it has been actualized by an event, which may be anticipated or unexpected. In Mbiti's words, Time is a composition of events, and since the future events have not occurred, the future as a necessary linear component of Time is virtually absent. Such is either *Potential Time*, with certainty of its eventual realization, or *No-Time* lying beyond the conceptual horizon of the people. The future has no independent existence of its own, since the events that compose Time have not occurred in it and once they occur, it is no longer future, but the Present and the Past. To Africans, Time has to be experienced to make sense.' This observation has led Mbiti to conclude that 'Africans Create Time.'[27]

Mbiti has attempted to link up African and Christian eschatologies: In doing this, he had identified five aspects of 'African eschatology' which may be 'profitably linked up with Christian eschatology.' Firstly, Mbiti has observed that in the African concept of history, there is no concept of 'The End.' For Africans, life is just a rhythm of the cycle of days, months and years, birth, initiation, death and so on.[28] In Mbiti's view, Christian eschatology maintains a belief in 'The End,' which is centred on Jesus Christ. Mbiti maintains that 'The End' is lacking in African eschatology. But in Christian eschatology we find it centred, as it is, in Jesus Christ; to this the New Testament bears witness . . . the New Testament is quite clear on this issue. According to its teaching, there is a 'Beginning' and there will be an 'End,' and the Incarnation introduces into this present life, the impact and the reality of the End-things.[29]

Having made this observation, Mbiti reiterates his suggestion that through the teaching of Christianity, Africans are being introduced into the future dimension of time. This is one of the major contributions of Christianity to African thought and life, according to Mbiti, the Incarnation has released into human history all the benefits of the Age to-Come, so that a new Creation is emerging and only the Consummation is awaited.

This fact introduces into African thinking both eternal realities and a future dimension of Time. It is not a future so much in terms of a distant goal simply to be hoped for and coveted, but a future dimension which is both present and future because its realities are eternal and cannot be exhausted in this life.[30]

Mbiti has come to the conviction that African religious heritage is only a preparation of the Christian Gospel and, therefore, it is not complete in itself. Though Africans have a monotheistic concept of deity, their religion is incomplete without Christianity.[31] As for the changes which traditional African life needs in order to be complemented by Christianity, Mbiti does not explain in great detail.[32]

According to Mbiti, although God has revealed himself to Africans, this revelation is a preparation for the Gospel and it will become complete, only in its encounter with Jesus Christ.[33] As observed above, Kihumbu Thairu,[34] William Ochieng, Okot p'Bitek and other East Africans question this view, which is held also by many Christian ethnologists.[35]

The second aspect which Mbiti considers in his attempt to link-up African and Christian eschatologies, is language. He notices that African languages 'lack' a future dimension of Time. According to him, 'Western education and modern national development plans are creating this new awareness in African thinking and life' but such education does not help the Church in answering the 'question of how to introduce meangingfully those eternal and eschatological realities which we find in the New Testament.'[36] Mbiti provides his own solution to the problem that suggests that Baptism and the Eucharist, when introduced into African religious life, will take care of the problem.

Without going into a full discussion of the matter it would seem that the Sacraments of Baptism and the Eucharist present themselves clearly as the areas where both temporal and eternal realities meet, and the media through which the temporal may catch glimpses of the eternal. The outward signs are performed and the elements handled in terms of the concrete and historical—water, bread, wine—elements that can be perceived through all the five senses of man. Through their sacramental use, these elements epitomize eternal realities. They are the nutshell of the Gospel, and dramatize before us the entire phenomenon of the Church from the Cross to the Parousia.[37]

By listing only two sacraments, Mbiti maintains his Anglican conviction, and implies a question on the conviction of African Catholic Christians and of those who do not practise the rite of Baptism with water and the Eucharist with bread and wine. Does it imply that such people would not be able to 'discover' the future dimension in this new way? Mbiti does not discuss this perspective of the question. But it raises the question as to whether Mbiti would accept as full

Christians, those who do not participate in the two sacraments which he has listed.[38]

The third aspect discussed by Mbiti is the African concept of 'The Hereafter.' According to him, 'The Hereafter in African thought is a natural form of immortality, with its life being a carbon copy of the present.' Contrasting this view with the Christian teaching about the Hereafter, he notices a radical difference. In Christianity, the hereafter is a life of the Resurrection.

The resurrection (Christian) is not a natural, mechanical and inevitable form of life but in reality, it is life resurrected to Life, real Life at its very source, the life whose nature and essential character are none other than 'everlasting,' 'eternal.' This is something entirely new to African thought since there is neither the World to come nor *eternal* as opposed to *temporal* realities.[39]

Mbiti continues to say 'To introduce eternal realities into African thought is to introduce something not only new, but revolutionary.' Although this is already being done, Mbiti is not satisfied with the way in which it is being done. It It is being done 'not in the most suitable, or even biblical form.'[40] His dissatisfaction arises from his observation that among many evangelists, the *Life to Come* is being promised as 'a *Utopia* in heaven where an essentially carnal life of pleasure and leisure replaces this present life of sorrow and pain.' In his answer to this brand of evangelization which Mbiti considers unsound, he advises that 'Sound evangelization must be rooted in a comprehensive and biblical christology.'[41]

Fourthly, Mbiti considers, the African sensitivity to the 'spirit-world' as an aspect of African life which 'could enrich the rather impoverished type of Christianity which has come to us through Western thought and practice, in which the spirit-world is either dismissed altogether or put in the extreme background—except for spiritist cults which function outside the Church.'[42] The way in which this enrichment may take place, is for the Church to learn from the African ancestor veneration how to establish a dynamic relationship between the departed and the living Christians. However, Mbiti does not say much about the relationship between African Christians and their non-Christian ancestors.

It seems that one of the reasons for the slackness in the veneration of Christian saints in Africa, is that most of the canonized saints were from an entirely different cultural, historical and political background. Whereas the English Anglicans may have a special attachment to St George, the Irish Christians to St. Patrick, and the Scottish Christians to St. Andrew, these saints have no emotional significance for the African Christians who belong to Churches established by missionaries from these respective areas of the British Isles.[43]

Samuel Kibicho has suggested that when Africans become Christians, they do not suddenly erase their traditional concept of their deity in order to accommodate the Christian God. Rather, they become Christians and add more attributes to their African deity, so that there is a continuity of faith.[44] This suggestion seems to be consistent with all voluntary process of acquiring new knowledge and new skills. Likewise, Africans ought not to be expected to make a radical break from their ancestral heritage, and to venerate saints who were canonized many centuries ago, many hundreds (or thousands) of miles from Africa, for reasons best known to the Christians who felt the impact of those canonized Christians.[45]

The fifth aspect discussed by Mbiti in his endeavour to link Christian and African eschatologies, is that of the separation, or estrangement, between God and Man. Mbiti argues that for Africans, this estrangement has never been resolved. He obtains his evidence from African mythology, which generally expresses Man's fall from favour with God, and the consequent suffering of humankind, but lacks any expression of a hope that this estrangement may in future be removed, so that humankind may enjoy paradise with God again. For Africans, humankind had only one chance at the beginning, but this chance was lost, and the situation will remain. In Mbiti's view, Africans have no myths about the culmination of history, but on the other hand, they have many myths about the primeval age, and the way humankind lived before suffering came into his experience. Concluding his discussion of this aspect, Mbiti has written that our (African) forefathers found no myths for the culmination of history however much they might have wished to find them. The New Testament supplies this missing link, not for the sake of mythology, but because the Incarnation makes it inevitable.

> We (Christians) have to transmit this message: Africa's broken rope between Heaven and earth is once and for all re-established in Christ. Africa's God who evidently withdrew from men to the heavens, has now come 'down' to man, not only as the Son of God, but also as Immanuel, God with us; and Death which came so early into man's existence, and from which there was no escape, is now for ever abolished.[46]

This view has been expanded by Malcolm McVeigh in his book, *Concepts of God in Africa*. Though McVeigh has concentrated on the concept of God rather than on the concept of Time, his conclusions are similar to those of Mbiti—among the main ones, there is the conclusion that traditional religions, Islam and other religious systems (are) preparatory and even essential ground in the search for the ultimate. But only Christianity has the terrible responsibility of pointing the way to that ultimate Identity, Foundation and Source of security.[47]

With such a premise, what is the possibility of 'dialogue' between Christianity and African heritage? It seems that African religions are often studied to expose their inadequacy, so that Christianity may fulfil that which the faith of African ancestors left unfilled. However, a more fundamental question may be raised, whether Christianity has *all* the answers, and explanations for the mysteries and challenges of life in which humankind is engulfed.[48] If Christianity has all these answers then what can one say about the perpetual divisions within Christianity? It seems that the answers of Christianity as it is understood in contemporary East Africa, and in the World as a whole are not as confidently conclusive as some Christians claim.[49]

There is considerable self-searching and self-questioning among some Christians, and in the words of Prof J G Donders, Christians *are not at home*—they are always on the way, *coming home*.[50] Christianity is a kind of a journey in which the committed Christian dedicates his life to his quest for home, and in whose teaching, to be at home is understood as being at one with God.

Having the foregoing survey of John Mbiti's scholarly interpretation of Christianity in contemporary East Africa, it is worthwhile to note what he himself feels about many of his critics. In an interview during the preparation of this study, Mbiti expressed his disappointment at the fact that many of those who do not agree with him offer only destructive criticism—they do not produce 'creative contributions' to the debate about Christianity. He expressed this concern in the following words:

> One may take note that my critics only attack—they do not produce creative contribution to the debate . . . and to me the contribution would be much more exciting than spending space, time and effort on tearing down what someone has constructed.[51]

The present study has had as one of its objectives, to explore what some contemporary East Africans have interpreted Christianity to be within the contexts of their own studies and experiences, with the hope that such an exposition might provide a basis for more creative contribution to the debate, for which John Mbiti has called.

Notes

1.   J S Mbiti, 'African Concept of Time' in *Africa Theological Journal, No. 1*, February, 1968.

2.   He has devoted a whole volume to this concept—*New Testament of Eschatology in an African Background*, London: Oxford University Press, 1971. In most of his scholarly works there is reference to this concept. See, for example, note 1 above.

3.   *New Testament Eschatology*, pp. 182–183.
4.   He has devoted a whole volume to a study of the concepts of God—*Concepts of God in Africa*, London: SPCK, 1970.
5.   Mbiti considers Okot's challenge unfair, because 'the categories as such are not Hellenistic. I have only used theological terminology to refer to them.' Interview with Mbiti, 6 December, 1975.
6.   *African Religions and Philosophy*, London: Heinemann, 1969, pp. 229-261: *Introduction to African Religion*, London: Heinemann, 1975, pp. 175-194.
7.   Interview with Mbiti, 6th December, 1975.
8.   Mbiti, *The Crisis of Mission in Africa*, Mukono: Uganda Church Press, 1971, p. 8.
9.   ibid, p. 8.
10. William R. Ochieng', 'Christianity and African Cultural Liberation', *Sunday Post*, 16 June, 1974.
11. The term 'pacify' is not mine. It was used to describe the expeditions which were organized by pioneer administrators to bring Africans to submission. It was used with the assumption that Africans were 'hostile' to the colonial pioneers. Historically, the missionaries may have arrived in some places earlier than the administrators and soldiers. But the effective establishment and spread of missionary work delayed until protection was provided by the colonial administrators.
12. A J Temu, *British Protestant Missions*, *op. cit.* pp. 91ff.
13. Ochieng', art. cit.
14. Kihumbu Thairu, *African Civilization*, Nairobi: East African Literature Bureau, 1975, p. 64.
15. ibid.
16. ibid. p. 68.
17. ibid. p. 68.
18. Okot argues that Christian Theology was established mainly through an extensive hellenization of Hebrew ideas. The religious ideas brought by the missionaries were so hellenistic that the Hebrew deity was not recognizable through them. In *African Religions in Western Scholarship*, Okot traces this development.
19. Johannes Verkuyl, *Break Down the Walls: A Christian Cry for Racial Justice*, Grand Rapids, Michigan: William B. Eerdmans, 1971, pp. 40-42.
20. K Thairu, *op. cit.* pp. 68-69.
21. See note above.
22. Okot p'Bitek, *African Religions in Western Scholarship*, p. 88.
23. J Mbiti, *African Religions and Philosophy*, p. 17. For more details on Mbiti's study of the African concept of time, read the same book pp. 15-28; *New Testament Eschatology in an African Background*, pp. 24-32. D B Barret (ed.) *African Initiatives in Religion*, pp. 17-28; Kwesi Dickson and Paul Ellingworth, (eds.). *Biblical Revelation and African Beliefs*, pp. 159-184, *Africa Theological Journal*, No. 1, February 1968, pp. 8-20; Mbiti, *The Crisis of Mission in Africa*, p. 3.
24. Kwesi Dickson and Paul Ellingworth (eds)., *Biblical Revelation and African Beliefs*, p. 159.

25. Mbiti, *The Crisis of Mission in Africa*, p. 3. However, Mbiti notes also that the 'discovery of future dimension of time' raised some challenges for the Church in contemporary Africa, such as the 'marked expectation of the millenium' which leads partly 'to the formation of small independent Churches clustered round a leader who symbolizes and partly fulfils this hope.' See *Africa Theological Journal* No. 1. February 1968, p. 20.

26. Mbiti, *The Crisis of Mission in Africa*, p. 3.

27. Mbiti, 'Eschatology' in Kwesi Dickson and Paul Ellingworth, (eds). *Biblical Revelation and African Beliefs*, London: Lutterworth, 1969, pp. 159-168.

28. ibid. p. 163.

29. ibid. p. 180-181.

30. ibid. p. 181.

31. In an interview, on 6 December, 1975, Mbiti suggested that he would not use the term 'incomplete' for African religions in the relation to Christianity: However, Mbiti has written:

> African traditional religions have a great deal in common with the teachings of Christianity in general. The reverse of this statement is not equally true. Christianity has much more than can be found in all of Africa's religiosity, notably the person of Jesus Christ and the witness which the New Testament bears of Him. The point however, is that practically all that African traditional background has can be found in Christianity in one form or another ("Christian Education in the Background of African Traditional Religions"), Nairobi, Paper presented to the CCEA 19 September, 1969, p. 1.

It is in this context that the term 'incomplete' is applied. This statement by Mbiti implies that African Traditional Religions are sub-sets of the greater set, Christianity.

32. In his discussion of the changes which the Church in contemporary Africa needs to undergo, Mbiti points out some shortcomings of traditional African life—inefficiency, shortsighted planning, lack of the spirit of experimentation. See *The Crisis of Mission in Africa*, pp. 3-4.

33. 'Christian Education in the Background of African Traditional Religion,' p. 1.

34. Kihumbu Thairu has further argued that the teachings of Jesus are not unique, and that they were taught in Africa and India long before Jesus was born. See *The African Civilization*, pp. 75-78.

35. For Example, Placide Tempels and his followers. Tempels in his *Bantu Philosophy* (p. 189) wrote: 'Christianity—and especially Christianity in its highest and most spiritual form—is the only possible consummation of the Bantu ideal.'

36. *Biblical Revelation and African Beliefs*, pp. 181-182.

37. ibid.

38. In an Interview with the author on 6 December, 1975, Mbiti made the following response to this comment on his selection of the two Sacraments:

> I am not questioning other Sacraments. I have only taken the two which make the kind of theological bridge which is concerned with eschatology. It is not possible to justify the same eschatological meaning in the other Sacraments ... I am not questioning who is or is not a "full Christian"—that is not my business.

39. *Biblical Revelation and African Beliefs,* p. 182.
40. ibid.
41. ibid. p. 183.
42. ibid. p. 183.
43. It is interesting to note that *African Christians* were not canonized as saints until very late in East Africa. Mbiti has not remarked on the canonization of saintly African Christians, a practice which might bring Christianity deeper into the African religiosity.
44. Samuel Kibicho, 'The Continuity of the African Conception of God into and Through Christianity: With the Kikuyu Conception of "Ngai as a Case Study." Paper presented to the University of Nairobi, Dept. of Philosophy and Religious studies Research Seminar on *Christianity in Independent Africa,* 14 January, 1975.
45. One of the basic principles of learning and teaching is that new insights and skills will be learned more readily if they are presented to the learner progressively, proceeding from what the learners know to what they do not know—building on past experience.
46. *Biblical Revelation and African Beliefs,* p. 184.
47. *African Religions and Philosophy,* p. 277.
48. Mbiti does *not* claim that Christianity has *all* the answers to human problems. But he maintains that it has the terrible responsibility of pointing the way to the Ultimate Identity (Jesus Christ) in whom all answers rest. (Interview, 6 Dec. 1975). See also, 'Christian Education in the Background of African Traditional Religions' p. 2
49. Some Christians, both African and expatriate seem to be very confident about their own norms of the expression of the Christian faith, to the extent of condemning others to Hell. Such a feeling was expressed by Byang Kato's response to a talk by Malcolm McVeigh in the Visitors' Programme, WCC 5th Assembly, Nairobi, 1 December, 1975. See also Byang Kato, *Theological Pitfalls in Africa*, Kisumu, Kenya: Evangel Press, 1975.
50. J G Donders, A talk presented to the Research Seminar on *Christianity in Independent Africa*, Department of Philosophy and Religious Studies, University of Nairobi, 13 January, 1975.
51. Interview, 6 December, 1975. Mbiti had reiterated this response in the second edition of his book *African Religions and Philosophy,* London: Heinemann, 1989.

Chapter Six

OKOT p'BITEK

I am not a religious person—neither pagan nor Christian. I do not believe in gods or spirits—holy or evil. I do not believe that souls or ghosts exist. I do not believe in supernatural forces. I do not hold, as Cardinal Newman did, that theology or the knowledge of God constitutes the core of all learning. And yet, I strongly recommend and support the study of African religions in African universities.[1]

Unlike John Mbiti who writes his scholarly studies about African heritage on his own premise of a commited Anglican Christian, Okot p'Bitek responds to the writings of Christian anthropologists and scholars on one hand, and to African heritage on the other founding his whole enquiry on the premise of a non-religious person.[2]

Okot's interest in the study of African heritage, is based on his interest to understand Africans, so that he may appreciate their beliefs and their presuppositions, and having understood them, 'serve them better.' His study of African heritage is not 'knowledge for its own sake,' but knowledge for the fulfilment of a purpose. This purpose is the service of African peoples.

The religion of a people, according to Okot p'Bitek, is perhaps the most important aspect of their culture. What they believe governs their lives. It provides their 'world-view'—the general direction along which they live, and relate to each other and to the universe. It guides them in their conduct of war and peace. It is the basis of their behaviour towards one another. The knowledge of the religions of our people is the key to the knowledge of our culture. The aim of the study of African religions in an African university is to know our people. We need to know our people, so that we can serve them better.[3]

John Mbiti also agrees that African culture and religion are very important aspects of African life, but as a Christian, suggests that these should be studied for the purpose of fulfilling the 'mission of the Church.' Mbiti has written that 'there is nothing sinful about using our (African) culture to fulfil the mission of the Church in Africa'[4] This is one of the points at which Okot p'Bitek differs with Mbiti and other Christian students of African heritage. F B Welbourn, for example, suggest that as far as a committed Christian is concerned, his relationship to his cultural heritage, is this, that he is firstly a Christian, and only secondly an African. The majority of those, who call themselves Christian, may think that they have secure salvation. They may claim to be better English or better Baganda. But they have no doubt that their primary identity is in national or tribal terms. They are English or Baganda who happen to be Christian. Yet Christianity claims to be the recognition, and acceptance of an identity—a principle of human unity—which is more fundamental *in nature* than language or skin colour. It is, therefore, hardly surprising if both individuals and groups insist, from time to time, on breaking away from the accepted compromise. Before anything else, they are Christians.[5]

Okot, and other cultural nationalists, reflect on their premise, that people are first what their heritage has made them to be, and secondly, they are what they choose to be. So, Okot cannot write-off his own cultural and religious heritage, although he has chosen to be an atheist. He is conscious of the fact that the majority of members of his ethnic community, the Acholi of Uganda, have a cultural and religious heritage which has been the foundation of their society. For Okot, Christianity is foreign to Africa, and although it is founded on Joshua of Nazareth, it was shaped and organized in the Graeco-Roman setting, and used first by the Roman empire and later by European colonial powers, to justify imperialism and colonization.[6]

In *Song of Lawino*, Okot illustrates how Africans, through the teaching of Christian missionaries, have come to look down upon their own heritage, upon their own past. They have been taught to be ashamed of the religion, culture and history of their own people, to the extent of accepting the myths which the agents of colonization used, to justify their 'occupation' and 'partition' of Africa. The Africans who have imbibed the teachings of the Mission School, have become, according to Lawino, the mouthpieces of those who 'civilized' Ocol. The missionaries were responsible for brainwashing Africans and preparing them for their role as drawers of water and hewers of wood for the colonial masters. *Song of Lawino* exposes in very clear words the impact of missionary education. The following are only a few of Lawino's words, to illustrate this:

> My husband (Ocol) treats me roughly.
> The insults:
> Words cut more painfully than sticks:
> He says my mother is a witch,
> That my clansmen are fools
> Because they eat rats,
> He says we are all Kaffirs.
> We do not know the ways of God.
> We sit in deep darkness
> And do not know the Gospel,
> He says my mother hides her charms
> And that we are all sorcerers.[7]

Later in the Song, Lawino continues to expose the attitudes of her husband, Ocol, with regard to Christianity:

> My husband (Ocol)
> Looks down upon me;
> He says
> I am a mere pagan,
> I do not know
> The way of God.
> He says
> I am ignorant
> Of the good word
> In the Clean Book
> And I do not have
> A Christian name
> Ocol dislikes me
> Because, he says,
> *Jok* is in my head
> And I like visiting
> The diviner-priest
> Like my mother.[8]

In *Song of Ocol*, Okot illustrates how the African products of missionary
education have come to justify the degradation of their own heritage, and to
abandon their own kith and kin on grounds of ignorance, illiteracy, backwardness
and such derogatory descriptions. Ocol absorbed from the mission-school more
European culture than Christianity. His justification of his own attitude towards
Lawino, does not explain his Christian bias. As far as Ocol is concerned, he is first
a 'civilized' person who has imitated his European master to the better, and only
secondly is he a Christian. Though F B Welbourn suggests that this should not be
the ideal expression of Christianity, it is what the likes of Ocol understands to
be Christianity. In his Song, Ocol regards himself as a true beneficiary of Africa's
independence, because he is 'educated' and 'civilized.' As for the heritage of his
own people, that for him is a drawback to progress, and it must be wiped away if it
has not been already abandoned or forgotten:

> To hell
> With your Pumpkins
> And your Old Homesteads,
> To hell
> With the husks
> Of old traditions
> And meaningless customs.
> We will smash
> The taboos
> One by one
> Explode the basis
> Of every superstition
> We will uproot
> Every sacred tree
> And demolish every ancestral Shrine.[9]

Lawino does not declare war against Ocol or his masters. All she asks is that she
should be left alone, to live with her own traditions, and modify them if she feels it
is necessary to do so. But Ocol is impatient and very militant against Lawino and
her old ways. By exposing these two positions, Okot p'Bitek has illustrated the
contribution which Christian missionaries and their African followers made to the
destruction of the African religious heritage during the colonial period. Though

the example of missionaries who Okot selects for illustration in his criticism of both Protestant and Catholic work among the Acholi may not be normative of the missionaries in East Africa generally, his assessment of the missionary work is conclusively negative, as shown in his books, *African Religions in Western Scholarship*[10] and *Religion of the Central Luo.*[11] In the former he shows that the missionaries came with two main objectives: to spread the gospel; and to 'civilize,' Africans.

According to Okot p'Bitek, the Christian mission to Africa was double-edged. The Missionaries came to preach the gospel as well as to 'civilize' and in their role as 'civilizers' they were at one with the colonizing forces: indeed they were an important vehicle of Western imperialism, which readily lent to the Churches its wealth.[12]

Okot quotes Thomas Beetham, a British Methodist missionary who confessed, as missionaries have occasionally done, that 'with the partition of Africa following the Berlin Conference, European rule began to provide an umbrella of law and order for missionary activity. A settled government, the telegraph, the railway—all helped.'[13] The word 'confessed' is used in this context because, in the midst of African criticism of missionary collaboration in the process of colonization, some missionaries have tried to over-emphasize their differences with the colonizing powers, in order to show that they meant no harm to Africans. Okot warns Africans against these 'tactics' of missionaries in contemporary Africa. The attempt to treat the missionary enterprise apart from the process of colonization, is interpreted by Okot as a tactic to ensure that missionary work continues under the guise of what Okot refers to as 'Dialogue with Animism.' The changed situation has forced the missionaries to review their tactics. There is, for example, the attempt to extricate Christianity from its past historical association with Western political, economic and culture aggression.[14]

Okot quotes M A C Warren to illustrate this point, and suggests that the arrogance which characterized missionary enterprise during the colonial period is being tactfully changed into a strategy of humility, in order to tame 'widespread revolt against any form of domination by the West.'[15]

In his other book, *Religion of the Central Luo*, Okot exposes through his case-study of the Central Luo, the misinterpretations which missionaries and anthropologists made about this people. Aidan Southall, in his introduction to the book, has written that this book *(Religion of the Central Luo)* fills important gaps in our knowledge of the Luo people. It gives for the first time an intelligible account of the position of the Paluo in Bunyoro, thus clarifying many aspects of the Nilotic involvements of the Bito and an excellent exposition of Luo ritual practices and beliefs in Acoliland.

'I (Southall) happen to agree with Okot's corrections of Crozzolora's ethnographic interpretations, and of Girlin's views of the relations between Acoli and Banyoro rulers, as well as recognizing his account of the connection between the Paluo and neighbouring Nilotic groups as sounder than my own (Southall's) when I was writing of them in relation to the Alur some years ago.'[16]

The two scholarly books, namely, *African Religions in Western Scholarship* and *Religion of the Central Luo*, help to affirm the conclusions Okot has arrived at in his studies, the conclusions which he expresses in the preface of *African Religions in Western Scholarship:*

> In this book I trace the study of African religions by Western scholars from the classical times of the present day. Two major conclusions are reached. First, that whereas different schools of social anthropology may quarrel bitterly over *methods,* they may all share the same view that the population of the world is divisible into two: one, their own, 'civilized,' and the rest, 'primitive.' The second conclusion is that Western scholars (including Christian ones) have never been genuinely interested in African religions *per se.* Their works have all been part and parcel of some controversy or debate in the Western world.[17]

In his songs, *Song of Prisoner and Song of Malaya,*[18] Okot p'Bitek illustrates in greater detail than in the *Song of Lawino,* the mess into which Africans have been plunged into by the 'new religion'—Christianity and the 'new order' founded by colonization. Both Lawino and Ocol, have become prisoners of the new situation. Lawino is unable to live according to the heritage of her people, although she wants to do so, and although she has the will power. On the other hand, Ocol has realized after *Uhuru* that he cannot become an equal to his previous colonial master to whose values he aspired. In the midst of this frustration, the illiterate people in the rural areas, represented by Lawino, resort to the local beer brewed in the traditional way.

Thus, Okot interprets the situation of society in contemporary East Africa and in Africa as a whole, as a kind of prison, in which everyone is a prisoner. The four songs published by Okot are a comprehensive social commentary on the joys, sorrows, hopes and fears of the East African rural, urban, employed, unemployed, literate and illiterate, population. *Song of Lawino* shows the joys of rural life, and exposes the weaknesses of such academically educated people as Ocol. *Song of Ocol,* on the hand, expresses the joys of the new acculturation, and exposes the weakness of Lawino's rural, illiterate background.

Ocol boasts of having become a Christian, although he does not comprehend fully the historical circumstances which made Christianity spread to the Roman Empire, the causes of the Reformation which gave birth to modern Euro-American denominationalism and the interests which motivated the missionarises to come to East Africa, and to the other parts of the Western empires. Ocol, is so blinded by the inventions of the West, that he cannot see the link between missionary interests and the interests of colonialists and imperialists. Ocol does not say whether his acceptance of Christianity is genuine, or is merely based on some ulterior interests such as the acquisition of academic education which is a guarantee for employment, and which had to be provided by the Christian missionary enterprise according to the master-plan of imperialism.

If Ocol's acceptance is genuine, then Lawino sees Ocol as a fool, because of his failure to see that his acceptance of the new religion, (Christianity) means at the same time the denouncing of his own cultural heritage, and the acceptance of Euro-American cultural norms. If Ocol accepts Christianity in order to get the material benefits provided by the Christian missionary enterprise to bribe the African converts, then Ocol is not really a Christian, but a pretender or a hypocrite according to the teaching of Jesus as recorded in the Sermon on the Mount. In either possibility, Ocol's position is weak. But Lawino's weakness is also exposed by her inability to cope with the new situation.

Nevertheless, Ocol has the advantage of being more able to identify himself with the new situation, despite the fact that he is not accepted completely into the company of the white foreigners who controlled the destiny of Africans in the colonial period. Christianity is part of this new situation, and makes no sense to Lawino who has refused, or been overtaken by, the establishment of Christianity and colonialism. In the new situation, it is fashionable to become a

Christian, and Ocol wants to be in fashion.

Song of Malaya takes this social commentary further. Malaya corresponds with Clementina in *Song of Lawino* and *Song of Ocol*. Her character, aspirations, and fears do not feature prominently enough in the two earlier songs, and Okot, therefore, devotes a whole poem to Clementina, to see the challenges of contemporary East African Society from the perspective of an academically educated, fashionable woman.

The social commentaries from the perspectives of Lawino and Clementina are aspects of one complex social situation. Both Lawino's and Clementina's commentaries are real to the contemporary East Africa situation and to Africa as a whole. Further, *Song of Prisoner* completes Okot's comprehensive social commentary on the contemporary East Africa Society. In *Song of Prisoner*, Okot emphasizes again and again that all of us are prisoners of the new situation, with all its complexities. Prisoner realizes his prison situation, as everyone realizes that belonging to a society inevitably conditions an individual to come to terms with the limitations imposed directly or indirectly by that particular society in a particular historical period and geographical location. Both men and women are prisoners of the new situation. Muthoni Likimani illustrates this view in *What Do Men Want?*

Thus Ocol and 'Prisoner' are aspects of that same complex social situation in which Lawino and Clementina have to live. Okot is very concerned about the necessity to comprehend the contemporary East Africa society in all its complexity. Witchcraft and Christianity co-exist, and often the people who have apparently become acculturated into Euro-American life-styles, resort to witchcraft and other beliefs and practices of Ocol's world, in order to meet immediate material needs. Many academically educated Africans still fear the traditional African beliefs, such as witchcraft, even when they have declared themselves Christians.

Song of Prisoner is a poem which exposes the frustrations of all the various sections of African society. Among other things, Prisoner sings a stanza of his social commentary as follows:

> I plead sickness,
> I am an orphan,
> I am diseased with

> All the giant
> Diseases of society,
> Crippled by the cancer
> of Uhuru.
> Far worse than
> The yaws of
> Colonialism
> The walls of hopelessness
> Surround me completely,
> There are no windows
> To let in the air
> of hope.

Uhuru (independence) has not fulfilled the expectations of the people. Yet, this lack of satisfaction has put people of all classes, creeds, clans and races into a prison-like situation which makes it impossible for anyone to act, except sing songs of sorrow. But if Prisoner feels this way, what of Christians? Are they prisoners also? Why should they be prisoners while Jesus preaches liberation? Are Christians also prisoners?

Okot's answer is positive. The liturgies and ritual practices in the Church are foreign to the cultural heritage and religious thought of the Africans. Though there are African bishops and priests, they also have been caught up by the 'wind' of change, by the tide of nationalism. At the same time they echo the slogans of nationalism, and continue with the liturgies, hymns, rituals, administrative structures, vestments and buildings inherited from the era of colonialism and the missionary enterprise. In this sense, the Christians are in an even more difficult prison situation than other members of the East African society. Thus, prisoner cries out:

> Cut off this rope
> Free my hands and feet
> I want to go to the Church
> And receive Holy Communion,
> Our black nationalistic bishop
> Will bless me
> With the holy water.

In this stanza, Prisoner alludes to the 'Freedom of Worship' which is respected in the Declaration of Human Rights but which is meaningless for African Christians who have followed the footsteps of foreign missionary fathers of the African Churches. The irony of this stanza is that Prisoner pleads to come out of one prison cell into another. The Church, though apparently free, is still not really free in Okot's view, because it is still an image, reflection, shadow and imitation of the respective denomination of which the founding missionaries although now it is headed by that nationalistic bishop. The bishop himself is thus a relic of a past era. Prisoner will, therefore, get no freedom into the Church, even though there might be freedom of worship.

The language of the Church is itself foreign, even to Prisoner, as will be indicated by the contrast provided in the stanza on African rituals of cleansing where there is no Holy Communion, no bishops, no holy water. Cleansing in the Church is done by one man, called a bishop. The cleansing ceremony according to Prisoner's custom, is an affair of the whole clan with men and women, ghosts and goats, spears and blood. Therefore, the Church provides no freedom of worship, no corporate sharing as that shared in African religious heritage. The administration of the ritual of cleansing is the monopoly of the bishop and his priests in the Christian Churches—but in the African ritual everyone, young and old, men and women, has an appropriate role.

I want to go to the village
To perform
The cleansing ceremony
To deaden the sharp spear
Of the vengeful ghost.
Let the elders gather
At the Clan Shrine,
Let them Spear
A black billy goat
And pour its blood
On the village pathway
I will step on the blood
And smear it on my feet
As I enter the homestead.

The women will wail
Their welcome
My mother will spit blessing
On my forehead
And the Elder
Will cut the killer mark
On my back . . . !

Through the words of Prisoner, Okot provides the mirror through which individuals in various social and religious circumstances can recognize their own limitations and weaknesses. He exposes the absurdity of abandoning one's own religious heritage in order to adopt religious customs which were developed in a different historical setting, to meet the needs of a different society.

Without stating it explicitly, Okot in *Song of Prisoner* seems to offer an explanation for the high rate of drunkenness, among the academically educated Africans who, though apparently successful, have lost their cultural and religious roots in their rush to imitate Euro-American norms. Though acculturation is inevitable whenever two cultures come into contact, Okot seems to emphasize that Africans should not abandon their own heritage in favour of foreign values. Those who fail to meet this challenge become disillusioned in the end. They drink no longer to enjoy life, but to escape from the frustrations of the contemporary period. They hoped that *Uhuru* would bring back the freedom of cultural expression which they lost with the coming of Christianity and Western civilization, but now they realize that the elite who took over, represented by Ocol, only continued to follow the patterns which had been set by the colonial masters—missionaries, administrators and settlers. On the other hand, many of the elite have come to realize that their *Uhuru* aspirations, to become as good or better than their former masters would come to naught without the cultural foundations which Ocol and his clique were militating against.

Thus, the elite finding themselves in a *cul-de-sac*, and being ashamed of returning to their people in the rural areas, resorted to drinking imported beers, wines and spirits. Thus, those who used to be the guardians of *Uhuru*, in their unconfessed frustration, became prisoners of the situation they had helped to create. David Mailu's poem, *My Dear Bottle*, is a further expression of this frustration.[19]

In *Song of Malaya*, Okot p'Bitek exposes the consequences of rigid morality which Christian missionaries introduced with regard to marriage. Monogamy was introduced in a society where polygamy was allowed, and owing to the artificial norms within the new family of such people as Ocol, the family in fact breaks up, although the two partners remain together owing to the indissolubility of marriage and the impossibility of divorce according to the 'Christian' teaching as introduced by the missionaries. Prostitution, according to *Song of Malaya*, arises out of this situation. Both the husband and the wife of the new 'educated' Family which tries to adhere to the norms of the missionary Christianity of the colonial period are unfaithful to each other, and engage in extra-marital relations. The prostitutes, in *Song of Malaya*, plead that they should not be made the victims of a situation which they did not create. The prostitute, answering the apparently respectable and educated wife whose husband goes with her, says:

> But tell me, Sister,
> Do you think
> There is something wrong
> With your husband.
>
> That he need
> Have only one woman
> For the rest of his life?
>
> Do you feed him well?
>
> Do you think he is
> Getting too fat?
> Does he not get
> Enough exercise?
>
> Has the doctor told him
> That he has a heart disease,
> And ordered him to sleep with
> Only one woman
> For the rest of his life?[20]

The songs which Okot has written are not merely poems. Okot has selected a medium of education and communication which was of central value in pre-colonial Africa, and he has used that medium to serve a similar purpose in contemporary Africa. That medium is poetry. Okot has pointed out in *Africa's Cultural Revolution*, that *Song of Lawino* was written first in his vernacular, before he translated it into English.[21] In pre-Colonial Africa, Oral Literature served the purpose of a social commentary. The poet was a social commentator who helped the leaders and ordinary members of the society to see where they might be making mistakes in their social development.[22] For Okot, literature should serve the same role in contemporary Africa and the artists in Africa need not turn professional as in Europe and America. Artists in Africa, are social commentators who are committed to the healthy growth of their societies and nations, as the politicians and other nationalists are. In this respect, African novels and poetry are not just 'art for art's sake.' They are not meant 'just for entertainment.' They also serve an educational function. Okot's songs are, therefore, part of his contribution to the discussion about religion and culture in East Africa. Much study was put into the preparation of the Songs, especially, *Song of Lawino* and *Song of Ocol*, and this is evident from the references which Okot makes to Acholi customs in *Song of Lawino*, and to the African writers such as Senghor, Nkrumah, Nyerere and others, in *Song of Ocol*.

Okot p'Bitek does not limit his criticism of Christianity to the work of the missionaries. He carries the criticism further to the Africans who have taken over, to carry on from where the missionaries left. Among these, Okot includes J B Danguah, K A Busia, W Abraham, E B Idowu, and John Mbiti.[23] He notes that the response of African students to the misinterpretations which missionaries and anthropologists made upon the African religious heritage, did not improve the situation. This was especially the case with regard to the study of African deities.

In the field of religious studies, Okot p'Bitek argues that African students have responded with a vigorous condemnation and rejection of the claims of Western scholarship which presented their peoples as 'primitive pagans.' But, instead of carrying out systematic studies of the beliefs of their peoples, and presenting them as the African peoples actually know them, the African scholars, smarting under the insults from the West, claimed that African peoples knew the Christian God long before the missionaries told them about it. African deities were selected and robed with awkward hellenic garments.[24]

In contemporary East Africa, Okot is at variance with J S Mbiti on this question about African deities. As far as Mbiti understands the subject, all the attributes of the Christian God, as expressed in Graeco-Roman terminology, are found in African religions. Africans conceive of God as Omnipotent, Omniscient, Eternal, Immanent, Transcendent, and so on. For Mbiti, there is only one God, and he is understood in the same way as the Christian God. The only difference is that the Jews have one name for him, the Greeks another, and as for the African peoples, each group has a name for the one God. The title of Mbiti's book (in this aspect of African religious heritage)—*Concepts of God in Africa*—makes his stand clear. In his later book, *Introduction to African Religion*, Mbiti does not modify this interpretation. He tries to simplify some of the terminology, by using familiar (English) words, but his position remains unaltered. The nature of God in African belief, according to Mbiti, is that God is *merciful, holy, all-knowing, present everywhere, limitless, self-existent,* the *First Cause, Spirit*. He never changes, *and is unknowable*. These attributes are found also in the Christian beliefs about God.[25]

This view which Mbiti maintains, is criticized not only by Okot, an atheist, but also by a fellow Christian, Byang H. Kato, who arrived at the conclusion that although the Jaba of Nigeria believe in a supreme being, their concepts are vague, and that being is not worshipped. Further, Kato disagrees with Mbiti's suggestion that Africa religions are *preparatio Evangelica,* that they are 'preparations for the Gospel' which finds fulfilment in Christianity. Byang H Kato, like Ocol in Okot's songs believes that the best thing for an African to do, is to cut himself completely from his heritage, and become a 'Bible Believing Christian.' The Christian Scriptures, as far as Kato is concerned, are adequate sources of the norms which a contemporary African Christian should use to conduct his own life.[26]

Okot p'Bitek, on the other hand, suggests that there is no point of comparison between the Christian God and the African deities. In his view, the Christian God appears to Africans just as another deity or spirit within the belief system of a people. This is how he explains the fact that many Africans become Christians and find no contradiction between their acceptance of the new faith, and their continuation of belief in their own heritage.[27] To Samuel Kibicho, this situation arises because Africans carry their concept of God along with them when they accept Christianity. So there is continuity of belief, though this continuity cannot be described as 'progressive revelation,' which is implied by Mbiti's notion of *preparatio Evangelica*. [28] Apparently to Okot p'Bitek, the Christian God is not important enough to warrant much attention from African scholars. In his conclusion of *African Religions in Western Scholarship*, Okot expresses this view in the following words:

> It seems to me that the new God of Christianity was taken by many African peoples as just another diety, and added to the long list of the ones they believed in. So that many African Christians are also practitioners of their own religions. [29]

He cautions African scholars, that 'the aim of the study of African religions (ought to be) to learn what Africans believe, and not to discover the Christian God in African beliefs.' This is his greatest concern, that Christians, both African and foreign, have used their studies of African heritage for purposes which are not in the interests of Africans, but which serve to alienate Africans, further from their own cultural roots. He offers the following caution:

> To assume before the start of our enquiry that Africans believe in a High God will lead us to look for evidence to support our thesis, will lead us to organize our facts in such a way as to prove our hypothesis. African deities have played the role of mercenaries long enough. The time has come to treat them with the respect they deserve; let us make them the sole objects of our enquiry. [30]

Whereas Mbiti views Christianity as an agent of positive change, Okot p'Bitek views it as one of the greatest hindrances for Africans to realize 'The *Uhuru.*' Okot notices that there are some African values which differ very much from those of Christianity, therefore, it is impossible to encourage the establishment of Christianity among Africans without at the same time forcing them to abandon their cultural and religious heritage. Christianity has been used throughout the history of the Western world since this religion was established and its aggressive strategy has not ebbed. During the colonial period it was used to justify the subjugation of the Africans by their masters, and after *Uhuru*, new tactics have been devised in the guise of 'dialogue with people of other faiths,' in order to continue the old prejudices, and maintain the supremacy of the Western world.[31] This seems to be Okot's biggest criticism of Christianity in contemporary East Africa. As far as his studies show, Christianity cannot be meaningfully interpreted in contemporary Africa, out of the context of colonialism, and Africa's struggle for total liberation. The last paragraph of Okot's *African Religions in Western Scholarship* emphasizes this position. The most critical decisions which leaders of Africa must take lie *not* so much in the economic or political fields, but in the fields of culture and of basic human values. Of course, there are conflicts between political philosophies and economic system(s); there is also the rivalry between power blocks. But the basic conflict is between fundamental assumptions and Western civilization and the fundamental assumptions of Africa civilization. The assumptions of the Western man have their roots in Judaism, the Greek and Roman experiences, the Christian faith and industrialisation. True *Uhuru* means the abolition of Western political and economic dominance from Africa and the reconstruction of our societies on the basis of African thought systems. The study of African religions is one important way of understanding African ways of thought.[32]

Okot p'Bitek is convinced that contemporary African society needs the talents and potentials of all its members in order to regenerate itself politically, religiously, economically, aesthetically in every aspect of life. With regard to artists, poets, creative writers and scholars, he emphasized in an interview that the moment a writer begins to write, he has already realized that he has a contribution to make for the improvement of his society. The same case applies to all other people who engage their efforts in creative activity. The taste of nation-building is, therefore, not the prerogative of politicians and businessmen (or any other interest groups) exclusively. Rather, it is the corporate effort of all the members of the society, so that each contributes what he feels best able to offer. It is with this in view, that Okot has taken pains to study the social commentary of the blind Acholi poet, Adok-Too. In spite of his blindness, his ability to entertain while at the same time educating his own people about their own selves, ought to become an indispensable contribution to nation-building.

Literacy ought not to be regarded as the basic criteria for determining the useful and the useless members of the society with regard to the contributions they can make to improve that particular society. After all, Okot argues, even Jesus of Nazareth, who began a movement that has influenced the world for twenty centuries and more to come, did not write his own social commentary on his contemporary society. Yet he made a great impact on both the Jewish community and the Roman authorities of his time.

According to Okot p'Bitek, to stick to the narrow dictionary definition of the word 'literature' is to accept the biased and one sided conception of the Western intellectuals, who defend it in that way to suit their interests. Writing, like painting and sculpting, is merely a tool that is used for 'communicating' ideas. As the painter uses brush and colour and surface (whether it is canvas or the wall of a cave), and the sculptor uses chisel and wood or stone, to produce shapes or images, the poet uses words. And the words may be spoken, sung or written. And a song is a song whether it is written or not. Jesus Christ sang many songs, but, although he could read, he did not write his songs on paper (or parchment or papyrus). The only piece of writing that the Nazarean ever did was in the sand!

Thus Okot considers Jesus to have been a social commentator who contributed to the self-understanding of his own society, and emphasizes that the role of creative artists of every form should be duly acknowledged in contemporary East Africa. Christianity as it was introduced by the missionary enterprise has not fostered the spirit of self-understanding, in Okot's view, because Christians have been too preoccupied with foreign concepts and irrelevant rituals, to bother about their own religious and cultural heritage.

Okot maintains, and I agree with him, that self-understanding cannot be achieved unless a person comprehends the beliefs and customs of his people, among whom he has grown and learned to be a social being. He challenges African Christians, both clerical and lay, to show in thought and action how relevant their faith is to the heritage of Africa and to the needs of contemporary Africans. Okot does not insist on a return to ancient and forgotten African beliefs and customs. But he insists, that for Africans to diagnose and comprehend their present problems and, therefore prescribe relevant, effective and meaningful solutions, they must understand the totality of their past and present. This is a complex undertaking and hence, Okot's call for each person's efforts to be involved and duly acknowledged.

NOTES

1. Okot p'Bitek, *Africa's Cultural Revolution,* Nairobi: Macmillan, 1973, pp. 85-86.
2. ibid.
3. ibid, p. 86.
4. J S Mbiti, *The Crisis of Mission in Africa,* Mukono: Uganda Church Press, 1971, p. 7.
5. F B Welbourn, *East African Christian,* Nairobi: Oxford University Press, 1965, pp. 12-13.
6. Okot p'Bitek, *African Religions in Western Scholarship* Nairobi: East African Literature Bureau, 1970, *passim.*
7. *Song of Lawino, and Song of Ocol,* p. 38.
8. ibid. p. 110.
9. *op. cit.* p. 209.
10. See note 6 above.
11. Okot p'Bitek, *Religion of the Central Luo,* Nairobi: East Africa Literature Bureau, 1971. pp. 41-58.
12. *African Religions in Western Scholarship.* p. 54.
13. ibid.
14. ibid. p. 56.
15. ibid.
16. *Religion of the Central Luo,* Introduction,
17. African Religions in Western Scholarship, p. viii:
18. Okot p'Bitek, *Two Songs: Song of Prisoner* and *Song of Malaya,* Nairobi: East African Publishing House, 1971.
19. David Maillu, *My Dear Bottle,* Nairobi: Comb Books, c. 1973.
20. *Song of Malaya,* pp. 151-152.
21. *Africa's Cultural Revolution,* p. 44.
22. ibid.
23. *African Religions in Western Scholarship,* pp. 47, 88; *Africa's Cultural Revolution,* p. 90.
24. *African Religions in Western Scholarship,* pp. 46-47.
25. cf. ibid. p. 88, J S Mbiti, *Concepts of God in Africa* S P C K, 1970.
26. Byang Kato, *Theological Pitfalls in Africa,* Nairobi: Evangel Press, 1975.
27. *Religion of the Central Luo,* pp. 40-58, *African Religions in Western Scholarship,* p. 113.

28.   J S Mbiti, *New Testament Eschatology in An African Background*, London: Oxford University Press, 1971, p. 189. In a lecture, Mbiti addressed to the Christian Churches Educational Association (Kenya) in Nairobi (19 September, 1969) he suggested that Christianity should be presented as the fulfilment of that after which, in all its richness, African religiosity has groped. This suggestion is supported by Ronald Dain. See R Dain and Jac Van Diepen, *Luke's Gospel for Africa Today*, Nairobi: Oxford University Press, 1972, p.6.

29.   See note 27 above.

30.   *Africa's Cultural Revolution* p. 91.

31.   Okot opposes this strategy because to him, it is a disguized approach to deal with 'animism.' See *African Religions in Western Scholarship*, pp. 52-58 Discussion on 'Dialogue with people of other faiths and ideologies' was conducted during the WCC 5th Assembly in Nairobi, and there seemed to be more openness on the part of Christians than there has been in the past. However, it is lamentable that there were no practitioners of African religions to speak for themselves.

32.   *African Religions in Western Scholarship*, p. 119.

Chapter Seven

NGUGI WA THIONG'O

> We went to their Church. Mubia, in white robes, opened the Bible. He said: Let us kneel down to pray. We knelt down. Mubia said: Let us shut our eyes. We did. You know, his remained open so that he could read the word. When we opened our eyes, our land was gone and the sword of flames stood on guard. As for Mubia, he went on reading the word, beseeching us to lay our treasures in Heaven where no moth would corrupt them. But he laid his on earth, our earth.[1]

Ngugi wa Thiong'o has been one of the most articulate critics of the Church in East Africa. Through his novels and short stories, he has tried to portray the impact of the Christian missionary enterprise on individuals and communities in Central Kenya. He has been particularly concerned about the co-operation and collaboration which existed throughout the colonial period between the missionaries, the settlers and the colonial administration. He does not try to oversimplify the relationship, and the self interest of each of these groups is clearly portrayed in the various characters whom he has created for his novels. For example, in *Weep Not, Child*[2] he describes the character of Mr Howlands, the settler who uprooted Ngotho from the land of his ancestors, and forced Ngotho and his children to become squatters on that same land. Howlands was not a missionary. He was a settle who was tied to the land he had acquired to the extent that the farm took the place of God in his life.[3] He even considered the farm to be more important than his wife.[4]

Mr Howlands daughter chose to become a Christian missionary, and her father considered her as lost. As far as he was concerned, there was no point in becoming a missionary.[5] He had come to Kenya to settle down on his farm, and have a territory which he could conquer, rule and command without interference. His cooperation with the colonial administration was necessary only when he needed the protection of the law and the forces to keep his squatters under control. For example, when the squatters organized a strike against Mr Howlands, he sought government action to discipline them. However, this resort to the colonial police came only when he realized that he was unable to control the strike through his own efforts. He did not want interference from anyone.

Mr Howlands called all his men. This was unusual. But he had not much to say because he did not want to waste time. He just warned them that if any man went on strike he would instantly lose his job. How could he allow a damned strike to interfere with any part of his farm? Even the government could not interfere with this. The blacks could agitate for anything. Such things were clearly affairs of the government—affairs that stood outside his *shamba*. And yet paradoxically, as the strike approached, he wanted a strong government action—an action that would teach these labourers their rightful places.[6]

Ngotho, the rightful land-owner who had been reduced into a squatter on the graves of his own ancestors, was also very tied to the farm. This was something which Mr Howlands never fully understood. Ngotho was tied to the soil because he was part of the land. Mr Howlands on the other hand, was tied to the farm because it symbolized his individual freedom. As far as he was concerned, only he and his farm mattered.[7] When Mau Mau came, he sent all his family back home to England, but he was left to see that his land remained in his ownership. He was fighting a lone battle for survival. In contrast, Ngotho's experience was the experience of his family, of his whole community. Although Ngotho hated Mr Howlands, he was not the one who killed him. Mr Howlands was killed by Ngotho's son, Boro. At that time, Mr Howlands' family was away in England. He had no defence.[8]

The daughter of Mr. Howlands chose to become a missionary for her own reasons, which were not known to anyone except herself. Her character is illustrative of the fact that Africans did not understand the real motives behind the missionary enterprise. What the Africans knew was that the missionaries' preachings were not consistent with their actions. Though there may have been a missionary who occasionally seemed genuinely interested in the welfare of Africans, in general and in practice, there was no clear distinction between the missionaries, the settlers and the colonial administrators. What Africans experienced was an apparently calculated strategy to destroy them and take their land by force.

Rosalind Mutua has analysed the self-interest of the Europeans in colonial Kenya, in contrast with the interests of Africans. She indicates that among the Europeans themselves there were occasional disagreements and frictions. But these disagreements were mainly with regard to who should control the African Community. The settlers wanted Africans to be labourers on the farms they had acquired; the missionaries wanted no interference in their plans to evangelize the Africans, and the colonial administrators wanted to run the colonies in as smooth and inexpensive way as was practicable.[10] This in practice meant that the settlers wished to pay very low wages or none at all. On the other hand, the administration was aware that strikes on the farms would lead to unrest in the colonies. The missionaries, while wanting freedom to spread Christianity without interference from anyone, at the same time wanted protection from the government. But this protection could not be given unless the missionaries saw to it that Africans, accepted the colonial masters. So it turned out that the schools, most of which were controlled by the missionaries taught Africans to read the Bible, and at the same time to sing the National Anthems of the colonial powers.[11]

Ngugi indicates throughout his writing that the situation in colonial Kenya was complicated by the fact that the Europeans, being strangers, had realized that they could not control the Africans unless they got some African collaborators. The Europeans, therefore, divided the African community, by singling out individuals who were to become instruments of colonization and civilization.[12] This strategy of divide-and-rule was adopted by all the three categories of Europeans in Kenya. The missionaries established mission-stations in which they indocrinated selected Africans to denounce their heritage, calling it primitive, heathen and satanic. The mission-stations became centres where clerks and office-messengers were trained to serve the colonial masters and the settlers.

When the Africans were made to understand that without book-learning, they could not survive in the new situation, they streamed to the missions to acquire the new learning. Most of them went to the mission schools not because they were attracted by Christianity, but because they needed book-learning which was gateway to employment on the farms, in the colonial offices and in the mission-schools.[13] Money had been introduced into the African communities where barter had been the traditional means of economic exchange.[14] In Ngugi's first three novels, *Weep Not, Child, The River Between,*[15] and *A Grain of Wheat,*[16] the main characters were all very committed to the conviction that only by acquiring European education, especially book-learning, could they lead their people out of colonial domination. This education was provided by the missionaries who in practice, proved to be agents of the colonial administration and suppliers of educated labour for the settlers' farms.

The missionaries needed evangelists to help in the spreading of Christianity. These African evangelists were alienated from their own community and from their own environment, and taught to look up to the missionary as the one through whom the African would get to heaven.[17]

Becoming a Christian meant imitating the ways of living of the missionary. But the missionary himself did not expose his culture completely to the African catechumens and catechists. For example, in the company of fellow Europeans, the missionaries talked, ate and joked as Europeans, while in the company of Africans they had to select and give to Africans what they considered simple enough for the 'primitive' Africans to understand.

One of the missionaries, Dr Irvine, a Presbyterian who worked in Meru, Eastern Kenya, wrote a small book called *How to Behave*. The book was a manual to show 'civilized' and 'Christianized' Africans should behave. In the book there were instructions on how Africans should behave in all circumstances, to show that they had become 'civilized' and 'Christians.'[18]

The evangelists, who were alienated from their own community by becoming imitators of European culture and followers of the instructions of the missionaries, became the main instruments which the missionaries used to spread Christianity.[19]

Ngugi's second novel, *The River Between*, shows clearly the polarization that resulted from this missionary strategy. In *The River Between*, Joshua was the character who accepted the teachings of the missionaries while denouncing the customs of his people. Initiation was a very important aspect of the life of the African community, and Joshua, after imbibing the instructions of the missionaries, rejected this aspect of his heritage. He commanded his daughters not to undergo initiation, at a time when this was a sensitive issue between the Africans and the missionaries. One of the daughters, Muthoni, wanted to be accepted as a mature woman by her community, and although she was the daughter of a Christian, she secretly underwent clitoridectomy, the form of initiation which was practised by the Agikuyu. A serious confrontation arose between the African Christians and the non-African Christians. Between these two groups was Waiyaki, who had acquired European education, and believed that with it he could lead his people from colonialism to freedom.

There were the Christians led by Joshua, 'the men of Joshua' as they were sometimes called. Their home? Makuyu. Then there were the people of the tribe, who had always been against the Mission and its faith. Kameno was their home base. The other ridges more or less followed this pattern. And so the ancient rivalry continued, sometimes under this guise or that guise. It was all confusion building up and spreading under the outward calm of the ridges.[20]

In this novel, Ngugi shows that Christianity, though it was claimed by the missionaries to be the sure way to heaven, brought only confusion to the African community. Rather than heal the wounds of disunity and cement the society, it broke up the African society into individuals who were concerned only with their own salvation as individuals and with their own small clubs of 'saved' Christians. The education which they brought to the Africans did not solve the problem either, because it concentrated mainly on uprooting the converts and learners from their social heritage. Waiyaki, though he had acquired European education, could not heal the hatred that existed between Joshua's men, the African Christians, and the rest of the community who had chosen to maintain the heritage of their ancestors.

Where did people like Waiyaki stand? Had he not received the white man's education? And was this not a part of the other faith, the new faith? The Kameno group was strengthened by the breakaway group lead by Kabonyi. Waiyaki felt himself standing outside all this. And at times he felt isolated.[21]

The negative role of the missionary enterprise is further illustrated in Ngugi's third novel, *A Grain of Wheat*. This is a novel which deals in detail with the Mau Mau, the culmination of all African efforts to resist the European invaders since the beginning of Kenya's colonization. The introduction of Christianity brought a spectrum of responses in the African community. Some were completely negative to the new faith, and so maintained the religious heritage of their forefathers. Chege in *The River Between* was such a person. He was Waiyaki's father. One day he took Waiyaki to the sacred place which had greatest religious significance in the community. Chege told Waiyaki:

> That is a blessed and sacred place. There, where Mumbi's feet stood, grew up that tree. So you see, it is Kameno that supported the father and mother of the tribe. From here, Murungu took them and put them under Mukurwe wa Gathanga in Murang'a. There our father and mother had nine daughters who bore more children. The children spread all over the country. Some came to the ridges to keep and guard the ancient rites.[22]

The community had its own religious myths about its origins. Those who rejected the teachings of the missionaries maintained their religious heritage, and lived according to the expectations of their ancestors. Chege took Waiyaki to the sacred grove as part of this traditional education. But Waiyaki was a child of the new age, the age of European colonialism. Though his childhood was rooted in the heritage of his ancestors, still he knew that he had to acquire a European education if he was to be an effective leader of his people.

Another response to the missionary enterprise was that of people who accepted the teaching of the missionaries unquestioningly. Joshua in *The River Between* was such a person. He accepted all that the missionaries taught, to the extent that he came to believe that for the colonized Africans like him obeying the colonial masters was an obvious duty. Joshua did not reflect on the implications of his acceptance of European supremacy and this angered the people of his community to such an extent that they rose against him. As far as he was concerned, he thought that his acceptance of Christianity was inseparable from his acceptance of colonial domination. Livingstone, the missionary who had taught him, was for Joshua not only the instrument of the Christian God to spread Christianity. He was also an instrument of God to spread 'civilization' to heathen Africans. He had been taught to believe that his fellow Africans were living in the darkness, and that the Europeans had been sent by God to bring light and order to a low primitive folk.

Hence, the colonial administrators were a part of God's plan for the salvation of Africans. When he (Joshua) learned that a colonial post was to be established in his area, he was not shocked. He thought this was right, and he tried to teach his fellow Africans to accept the new rulers and pay taxes to the sovereign of England. For Joshua, without colonization Africans would not be saved. But the unquestioning attitude of Joshua brought him into serious trouble with his fellow Africans.

Things had not gone well with Joshua. People at Kameno were becoming restless and believed that it was Joshua who was responsible for the white men who these days often came to the hills. There were rumours that a Government Post would soon be built at Makuyu and that the hills would be ruled from there. In his last visit, one of the white men had announced that people in these regions would begin paying taxes to a government in Nairobi. People shrugged their shoulders, not knowing what a tax was. Nevertheless, they blamed Joshua for this interference.[23]

Joshua, and those like him, were partly responsible for such developments, because the Europeans, settlers, administrators and missionaries alike had to rely on porters and guides who would be trustworthy and faithful to them. Joshua was convinced that the colonial government had come for the good of the Africans, so he did not care about the criticisms of his fellow Africans. In any case he thought that the Europeans would come to his aid if his life was in danger.

'Joshua did not mind . . . He himself knew what a government was, having learnt about this from Livingstone. He knew it was his duty as a Christian to obey the government, giving to Caesar the things that are Caesars and to God the things that are God's. That was what he wanted every Christian to do. And was the white man not his brother? Was the white man responsible for the ills of the land? No! It was the blindness of the people. People would not walk in the light. Look now at the preparations and rituals going on all over the land. Look at the sinners moving deeper and deeper into the dirty mind of sin. Moments of great anger sometimes came to Joshua. And he would remember he had to be patient. Prayers would soon work a miracle on the ridges. And so Joshua went on his knees. He prayed that the people should leave their ways and follow the ways of the white man.'[24]

Micere Githae Mugo has been very critical of this brand of Christian missionary teaching, which inculcated docility and passive humility in the African converts to Christianity. She has emphasized that the Christian Scriptures were used by the missionaries to facilitate easier colonization of Africa by the countries from which the missionaries came.[25] In her view, the Christian Scriptures were interpreted by the missionaries in such a way that the African converts misunderstood the character of Jesus, and lost the revolutionary zeal which led Jesus to defy the Pharisees, the Sadducees, the Scribes, the Herodians and the Zealots, for the liberation of his people. She regards Jesus as a hard-core revolutionary who was always on the side of the powerless and the oppressed, and maintains that the Gospel was distorted by those missionaries who wanted to keep Africans in an inferior position. The emphasis which the missionaries placed on passive humility and docility, leading the African converts to accept colonialism without question was a distortion of the true character of Jesus, in Micere Mugo's view.[26]

This view, coincides with the reaction of Joshua's neighbours in Ngugi's novel, although they did not analyse the Gospels in the way Micere Mugo has done. For example, Micere argues that Jesus, the man who was always on the side of the powerless, would not contradict himself by saying that 'if someone strikes you on the left cheek, give him the right one also.' Rather, she implies that the law Moses of 'An-eye for an eye' was superceded by Jesus with the teaching that 'if someone strikes you on the left cheek, *Crush* his right jaw.' Such a teaching would be considered with the character of Jesus, as Micere Mugo perceives it. Her interpretation of Christianity questions even the transmission of the Gospel, because in her view some of the sayings which are attributed to Jesus are not authentic and consistent with his character.[27]

A third response to the missionary enterprise was that represented by the character of Kabonyi in *The River Between*. There were some Africans who at first thought that the new faith was worth following, but later changed their minds when they realized that the teaching of the missionaries was more concerned with destroying the African heritage than with preparing Africans for heaven. These Africans took the Bible, read it and interpreted it in their own way. They found that the Hebrew life and religion as depicted in the Old Testament were akin to the African traditional life, and these (African) Christians used their Biblical understanding to interpret the events which dominated them in the colonial situation.

To such Africans, who formed 'African Independent Churches,' the Old Testament had a special significance. The deliverance of the Hebrews from Egyptian bondage by Moses became a motif which gave special meaning to the plight of the colonized Africans. The colonial masters were interpreted in terms of Pharaoh's ruthlessness and hardness of heart. What Africans needed, according to this new interpretation of colonial history, was a Black Messiah, a Black Moses.[28] It is interesting that for many Africans who read the Christian Scriptures in school, the Old Testament stories had greater significance than the abstract theological expositions of Paul in the Epistles. This may still be the case, through no research has been conducted regarding this question among African pupils. For Nyambura in *The River Between,* the concept of the Black Messiah was inseparable from her belief in Jesus Christ.[29] Though Waiyaki was not a committed Christian, Nyambura considered him as the only one through whom she could be saved. She loved him, and more than that, he was the saviour who would lead his people to liberation from the yokes of colonialism. He was her hope, and he was the hope of the community.

Day by day, she (Nyambura) became weary of Joshua's brand of religion. Was she too becoming a rebel. (Like her sister Muthoni)? No she would not do as her sister had done. She knew, however, that she had to have a God who would give her a fullness of life, a God who would still her restless soul; so she clung to Christ because He had died on the Tree, love for all the people blazing out from His sad eyes. She wished He could be near her so that she might wash and dress His wounds. She envied Mary, the Mary who had annointed the feet of Christ with oil. Even this did not always satisfy her and she hungered for somebody human to talk to; somebody who she could actually touch and feel and not a Christ who died many years ago, a Christ who could only talk to her in spirit. If only she could meet Waiyaki more often; if only he could stay near her, then Christ would have a bigger meaning for her. But Waiyaki was becoming important and he was on the other side. Perhaps they would remain like that, a big, deep valley separating them. Nyambura knew then that she could never be saved by Christ; that the Christ who died could only be meaningful if Waiyaki was there for her to touch, for her to feel and talk to. She could only be saved through Waiyaki. Waiyaki then was her saviour, her black Messiah, the promised one who would come and lead her into the light.[30]

Njoroge in *Weep Not, Child,* prayed to the God of Abraham, Isaac and Jacob, for the success of the strike which the squatters were planning against Mr Howlands. In his bed, he knelt down and prayed. 'God forgive me for I am wicked . . . O God of Abraham, Isaac and Jacob, help Thy children. Forgive us all. Amen. Lord, do you think the strike will be a success?'

He wanted an assurance. He wanted foretaste of the future before it came. In the Old Testament, God spoke to His people. Surely He could do the same thing now. So Njoroge listened, seriously and quietly.[31]

In his novels, Ngugi is sympathetic towards those who remained faithful to the true heritage of their ancestors. He is also sympathetic towards those who tried to relate the Christian Scriptures to the historical situation in which the Africans of the colonial period found themselves. For example, in *The River Between,* Muthoni, the daughter of Joshua, saw Jesus only when she had undergone initiation according to the custom of traditional community. Although she died after the operation, she believed that she had triumphed over death, because she died a mature woman.

She did not last many hours after they arrived in Siriana (Mission Hospital). Waiyaki could still remember her last words as they approached the hospital. 'Waiyaki' she turned to him, 'tell Nyambura I see Jesus. And I am a woman, beautiful in the tribe.'[32]

Though Ngugi does not say explicitly that Christianity should take root in Africa, Muthoni's character in his novel and the way she dies is indicative of this possibility. She went through the most important ceremony of her traditional community, initiation, and at the same time, in Christian theological terms, she triumphed over death through Jesus Christ. In her life, however, there was a link between Old Testament religion and New Testament theology, which was experienced practically in her own positive response to the demands of her social and religious heritage.[33]

Yet a fourth response to the Christian missionary enterprise is that which is represented by the Revivalists in *A Grain of Wheat* and in *Weep Not, Child*. The Revival movement started in Rwanda and spread through Uganda into Kenya. It reached Central Kenya around 1940, and was very active during the Mau Mau Emergency.[34] The Revivalists believed that it was not enough to be baptised as a Christian, or to be registered as a member of a particular denomination. The criterion for becoming a true Christian according to the Revivalists, was accepting Jesus Christ as your Personal Saviour.[35] The Revival movement was inter-denominational, but it was prevalent mainly among Anglicans and Presbyterians. The Revivalists were greatly persecuted during the Mau Mau emergency because they sided neither with the loyalists who yielded to the British colonial protection, nor with the African liberation movement. They had their own reasons for not joining any of these sides. They were not merely neutral. For them, Jesus Christ, the Son of God was their only Master, and they did not need to pledge loyalty or allegiance to any temporal power, be it Mau Mau or the British monarch.[36] As far as they were concerned, African traditions were heathen and satanic. They were the products of darkness.[37] Any Saved Christian was expected to abandon all his traditional heritage, and begin a new life 'in Christ.' The British colonial authority was also 'absolutized' and tended to imply that the loyalty of African subjects to the British Emperor was more important than the faith of Africans in God through Jesus.[38]

Members of the Revival Movement organized themselves into confessional fellowships, with a normative order of agenda. In each fellowship meeting, each attendant was expected to be a participant. Each member of, or visitor to, the fellowship was expected to give a testimony of his salvation, and the testimonies also followed a particular pattern. The Revival Movement established norms which are still followed by groups of Christians who call themselves "saved". Sociologically speaking, the Revival movement was a sect, but legally, it was not registered as such members of the Revival fellowship in each area remained members of their own church, but after the official worship services they would meet in the church building, in members' homes or in the open, to give their testimonies. One of their most prominent distinguishing marks, was and still is, oral confession and testimony.[39]

Members of the Revival Movement believe that a person is not a genuine Christian unless he gives oral testimony and confession to anyone he meets anywhere, at any time. They claim that their exclusiveness is based on the teaching of Christian Scriptures.[40] Ngugi records the form of the typical confession which a 'Saved' Christian would give in a fellowship meeting, or to anyone. In a *Grain of Wheat*, it was the testimony given by Rev Jackson Kigondu:

> I had called myself a Christian. I had put a white collar around my neck and thought this would save me from the fire to come. Vanity of Vanities. All was vanity. For my heart harboured anger, pride, jealousy, theft and adulterous thoughts. My company was with drunkards and adulterers. I had not seen Jesus. I had not found the light. Then on the night of January 1953, I was suddenly struck by the thunderbolt of the Lord, and I cried again: Lord, wash me in thy blood. And he said: Jackson, follow me.[41]

This is still the form which confession takes among the Revivalists, the 'Saved Ones.' After making this general confession, the member continues to enumerate the sins which he used to commit before he 'became saved.' The list is often quite long, there are 'sins' which will be mentioned by almost every Christian. These are eating, drinking and dancing with sinners, adultery, anger, jealousy, stealing, smoking, and lust for wealth. In Ngugi's novel, Jackson confessed that he had often failed to separate himself from the unbelievers—fellow members of his own village. He regarded himself as a 'Christian Soldier, marching to war.' For the revivalists, politics was dirty and sinful—a good Christian must keep out of it. A good Christian must not seek after material wealth, because Christians must lay all their treasures in heaven! This attitude and interpretation of Christianity is still prevalent among most revivalists, and inspired Henry Okullu to publish his small but relevant book, *Church and Politics in East Africa*.

Ngugi notes that 'the Revivalist movement was the only organization allowed to flourish in Kenya by the government during the Emergency.' To illustrate the plight of these and puritanical Christians, Ngugi included two incidents in his novels, *Weep Not, Child*, and *A Grain of Wheat*, respectively. In the first incident, Isaka, one of Njoroge's teachers who had become a 'Saved

Christian', was shot dead by the white military forces because they decided he was a Mau Mau. He had forgotten his identity papers while setting off for a revival fellowship meeting. At the spot where the fellowship was to take place, the military patrol hid, and they wanted everyone in the group to produce their papers.

Isaka squatted and calmly watched the scene. He had no documents. When the white soldier shouted at him, Isaka answered in a calm, almost resigned tone. Where had he left the documents? Satan had made him forget them at home. But the white soldier knew better. Isaka was a Mau Mau. Again Isaka replied that Jesus had saved him and he could not exchange Jesus with Mau Mau. The officer looked at him with reddening eyes. Yet he did not touch him. There was something strange in the teacher's calm. When the others were allowed to go, Isaka was made to remain. He did not protest. 'Come this way and we'll see what Jesus will do for you.'

He was led into the thick dark wood. Before the others had gone very far, they heard one horrible scream that rang across the forest. They dared not turn their heads . . . Suddenly there was one other scream which was swallowed by a defeaning report of machine-guns. Then silence.

'They have killed him,' one of them said after the report.[43]

The other incident is in *A Grain of Wheat*. Rev Jackson Kigondu, one of the revivalists, was killed not by white soldiers, but by his fellow Africans who considered him as one of the traitors of the struggle for African liberation. The leaders of the struggle did not see the possibility of a neutral or even a third position in their organization against the colonialists. As far as they were concerned, anyone living in the situation was either for the colonialists, or for the liberation struggle. Though Jackson claimed to be for Christ, leaders of the African struggle interpreted this to mean that Jackson was against them and, therefore, loyal to the British Empire and the colonialists. For them, loyalty to Christ was identical with loyalty to the colonial power, unless the African Christians were committed to the African struggle. But Jackson believed that he belonged to a third loyalty—he was loyal to the Kingdom of God, in heaven.

My home is heaven here on earth I am a pilgrim.

Brothers and sisters in the Lord rose and started singing and jumping about in the Church: Others went to the front and embraced Jackson and kissed him a holy kiss. Jackson tore the collar and his hat—a sign of humility and a heart broken to pieces by the Lord. His body was one morning found hacked with pangas into small pieces: His house and property were burnt to charcoal and ashes . . . News of

Jackson's death spread terror into peoples hearts . . . Who would be struck next by the Mau Mau, people wondered, remembering Teacher Muniu (another revivalist, also reputed to be a police informer) who had been killed in a similar method only a few days before?[44]

The revivalists maintained (and still maintain) that death was the gateway to heaven, and was therefore not a source of sorrow. This interpretation of death is illustrated by Ngugi's narration of the impact of Jackson's death on the members of his revival fellowship.

The revivalists praised God and said that Jackson and Muniu, by their deaths, had only followed in the footsteps of the Lord. What greater honours could befall a Christian?[45]

In his narration of these incidents, Ngugi hints at the factors that led to the vulnerability of the Revival Movement. Christians would be accepted as 'brothers and sisters in the Lord' only on grounds of oral testimony and confession. Keeping to the norms of the group meant that it was possible for the group to be infiltrated by people who were not genuinely 'saved' and these infiltrators could manipulate the group for their own ends. For example, in Weep Not, Child, Ngugi narrates that when Isaka was killed by the white soldiers, he had gone along with other 'brethren' for a fellowship in the woods. But the spot where the fellowship would have been conducted was surrounded by ambushing soldiers, armed with machine-guns. It is plausible that the spot had been recommended to the fellowship by a fellow revivalist who had contact with the forces, and was on the side of the oppressors.

In one of his later publications, Ngugi has tried to expose some of the weaknesses of Christian living in contemporary Kenya. He has done this in his collection of short stories, published under the title Secret Lives (1975). The collection is divided into three parts. The setting of the first part is the same as that of his first three novels, Weep Not, Child, The River Between and A Grain of Wheat. It concentrates on the importance of children in African life, and the difficulties of a childless woman in a traditional African family. The stories in this part do not add anything new to the subject of this study. However, Ngugi's sympathy with the African religious heritage, is made more explicit. For example, in the first story, a young woman who got married to an old man with four other wives failed to bear children, and the man became very hostile to her. The other wives, feeling jealous of a young additional wife in the family, found another cause to ridicule Mukami, the youngest wife. She was called Thata, a barren woman.

Mukami, having failed to get sympathy from anyone in the family or in the neighbourhood, turned to her religious heritage for refuge. She beseeched the deity of the Gikuyu to help her, and pleaded with her ancestors to remove her from her misery. In her desperation she wailed:

O spirits of the dead, come for me!
O Murungu, god of Gikuyu and Mumbi,
Who dwells on high Kerinyaga, yet is everywhere,
Why don't you release me from misery?
Dear Mother Earth, Why don't you open and swallow me up?
Even as you had swallowed Gumba—
the Gumba who disappeared under mikonge roots?[46]

In her desperation, Mukami decided to run away from the family and seek a place of refuge, a place where there could be peace and salvation. She found this at the sacred Mugumo tree. 'And she knew; she knew, that this was the tree—the sacred Mugumo—the altar of the all-seeing Murungu. Here at last is the place of Sanctuary, she thought.' Ngugi narrates the story of the woman's rush for the sanctuary in the following words:

> She ran, defying the rain, the thunder and the ghosts. Her husband and the people of Muhoroni Ridge vanished into insignificance. The load that had weighed upon her heart seemed to be lifted as she ran through the thorny bush, knocking against the trees, falling and standing up. Her impotence was gone. Her worries were gone. Her one object was to reach the tree. It was a matter of life and death—a battle for life. There under the sacred Mugumo she would find sanctuary and peace. There Mukami would meet her God, Murungu, the God of her people. So she ran despite her physical weakness. And she could feel a burning inside her womb. Now she was near the place of sanctuary, the altar of the most High, the place of salvation. So towards the altar she ran, no, not running but flying. For she felt light as a feather. At last she reached the place, panting and breathless.[47]

In this story, Ngugi shows that the African religious heritage provided a spiritual refuge for those who were in despair. John Mbiti and Malcolm McVeigh have suggested the contrary, and indicated that the problem of death and evil are unresolved in African religious heritage. In this story, and in other incidents narrated by Ngugi in his novels, Ngugi suggested that as far as Africans are concerned, it is not necessary to embrace a new foreign religion in order to gain spiritual satisfaction and peace. Christianity, therefore, is viewed as an imposition on African individuals and communities, an imposition which brought more harm than advantages to the African people. The breaking of traditions, the degradation of African rituals, and the breakdown of African family life, are some of the negative consequences of colonialism and Christianity, in Ngugi's analysis.

The second part of the collection is set in the Mau Mau period, and shows in greater detail the feelings of the Africans and settlers in the circumstances. In one story, the settlers cannot understand why Africans were killing their benefactors. Some of the settlers considered themselves missionaries of some sort, who were committed to civilize the Africans and show them the light. The squatters, on the other hand, knew that they were being exploited, and felt that they would never control their own destiny as long as the settlers continued to dominate them on their own land.

In the story, Ngugi emphasises his belief that the missionaries, the settlers and the colonial administrators were collaborators involved in the exploitation of Africans.

The third part of the collection definitely adds to Ngugi's reflections on Christianity in East Africa, especially in Kenya. In his preface to the book, Ngugi gives a clue as to what inspired him to write the stories entitled *Minutes of Glory*, *Wedding at the Cross*, and *Mercedes Wedding*. Ngugi had been out of his country for several years after publishing his three novels. On his return, he found a situation which inspired him to respond.

> In 1971 I returned to Kenya from a one year spell teaching African literature at Northwestern University in Evanston, Illinois. I looked at the tired and bewildered faces of the people: I went to places where people went to drown their memories of yesterday and their hopes and fears for tomorrow in drinking. I visited various bars in Limuru, drinking, singing and dancing and trying not to see or remember. A friend told of an interesting episode. A bar-maid had been arrested for stealing money from an aged trader, her one-night lover. The friend who told the story was condemning the rather petty and amateurish theft. But I was intrigued by the fact that the girl had returned to the same bar for a whole day lived in an ostentatious display of wealth and well-being. That was the beginning of the three stories (*Minutes of Glory*, *Wedding at the Cross* and *Mercedes Funeral*) which were meant to be first in a series of secret lives.[48]

In the first of these three stories, Ngugi narrates that the bar belonged to a Christian who was respectable and well-to-do. The proprietor not only exploited the bar-maids by overworking them, but he frustrated them by practising favouritism on one of the girls who had won his eye. She worked less, and was paid in kind. She had a room to herself, in the bar, while all the other girls had to sleep in the bar, in order to attract more male customers. In all this frustration, Beatrice, who had become a bar-maid out of despair from lack of employment, decided to take money out of the pockets of her one-night lover. The man, though a regular customer at the bar, was not accepted by the richer patrons, because he belonged to a lower social status, being a truck driver. When his money was taken, he summoned the police, and the girl was arrested. All the patrons became colleagues in condemning this girl, who took the money. The girl herself did not act as a thief. She took the money, and the following morning she used it to buy cosmetics and fashionable clothing, with which she would be able to show that she was a woman. She returned to the same bar that evening, only to be arrested for a theft she had committed the previous night. She did not resist. A fellow bar-maid behind the counter wept when Beatrice was arrested, while the drunken patrons laughed and grubled about 'these bar girls.'

In this short story, Ngugi tries to expose several weaknesses of Christian living in contemporary East Africa, especially in Kenya. Firstly, he notes that the bar was owned by someone who was accepted as a respectable Christian, while actually he was an exploiter of girls and frustrated men. He had no regard for them as human beings. He was only concerned with making money, and gratifying his lust. He was respected as a Christian apparently because he had money. Wealth and Christianity are closely linked, Ngugi seems to say. In sympathy with Beatrice who fell victim to this respectable Christian, Ngugi has written:

> She (Beatrice) worked in Ilmorog Starlight Bar and Lodging. Nyaguthii with her bangled hands, her huge-ear-rings, served behind the counter. The owner was a good Christian soul who regularly went to Church and paid all his duties to *Harambee* projects. Pot-belly, grey hair, soft-spoken. A respectable family man, well-known in Ilmorog. Hard-working even, for he would not leave the bar until the closing hours, or more precisely until Nyaguthii left. He had no eyes for any other girl; he hung around her, and surreptitiously brought her gifts of clothes without receiving gratitude in kind. Only the promise. Only the hope for tomorrow. Other girls he gave eight shillings a month. Nyaguthii had a room to herself. Nyaguthii woke up whenever she liked to take the stock. But Beatrice and the other girls had to wake up at five or so, make tea for the lodgers, clean up the bar and wash dishes and glasses.[49]

Nyaguthii had lost all feeling for being considered because she had been brought up in a very rigid Christian home. She made the confession of the emptiness in her life, to Beatrice, her fellow bar-maid. They were both victims of respectable Christian life. Nyaguthii, confessing to Beatrice and explaining that she did not hate her, made this disclosure of background. She was explaining why she had become a bar-maid:

> My father and mother were fairly wealthy. They were also good Christians. We lived under regulations. You must never walk with the heathen. You must not attend their pagan customs—dances and circumcision rites for instance. There were rules about what, how and when to eat. You must even walk like a Christian lady. You must never be seen with boys. Rules, rules all the way. One day instead of returning home from school, I and another girl from a similar home ran away to Eastleigh. I have never been home once this last four years. That's all.[50]

Ngugi seems to see a similarity between the proprietor of the Bar where Beatrice and Nyaguthii worked, and the parents of Beatrice. One of their common characteristics, is that the two men were wealthy, and were Christians. Ngugi seems to be questioning the compatibility between Christianity, wealth and respectability.

In the second story, *Wedding at the Cross*, Ngugi develops his questioning by narrating another case, that of Christian living among the poor African Christians. Miriam came from a family of squatters in the Rift Valley. Her parents were richer than most other squatters, and they were Christians. About Miriam's parents, Ngugi has written:

> Miriam's family was miles better-off than most squatters in the Rift Valley. Her father Douglas Jones, onwed several groceries and tea-rooms around the town. A God-fearing couple he and his wife were: they went to church on Sundays, they said their prayers first thing in the morning, last thing in the evening, and of course, before every meal. They were looked on with favour by the white farmers around; the District Officer would often stop by a casual greeting. Theirs then was a good Christian home and hence, they objected to their daughter marrying into sin, misery and poverty.[51]

But Miriam was determined to marry a young man from a much poorer family, and a less 'Christian' background. The parents objected to Miriam's annoucement that she wanted to wed Wariuki, her boyfriend. They advised her not to marry him, but she decided to do so, with or without her parents. When Wariuki went to Miriam's parents to seek approval for the wedding, this was the reply he received from her father:

> I say it again, we do not object to this union. But it must take place at the cross (Church). A Church wedding, Wariuki, costs money. Maintaining a wife also costs money. Is that not so? You and your head? Good. It is nice to see a young man with sense these days. All that I now want, and that is why I have called in my counsellor friends, is to see your savings account. Young man, can you show these elders your post office book?[52]

Miriam eloped with Wariuki, and her husband was employed by an Asian Timber Merchant. When the proprietor left the country owing to the termination of their trading licence, Wariuki became the proprietor, and he became a rich man almost overnight.

His character changed. He began to mistreat his workers, who only a short while before, were his colleagues. Much more important to our study, Wariuki became a Christian. Apparently, in Ngugi's view, every respectable person would have to be a Christian. Christianity has become a fashion, along with the acquisition of cosmetics and imported commodities such as cars, woolen suits, refrigerators and other luxury items.

Miriam had already adjusted her mind to live a simple life, the life of her husband's background. She did not like Wariuki's change of character which came from his acquisition of wealth. Wariuki, however, believed that he had to complete his respectability by becoming a 'full Christian,' and organizing a re-union with his in-laws. Now that he was rich, he could confront his in-laws.

He drove his expensive car with all his family to the parents of Miriam. The re-union was possible only because Wariuki had money and was a 'confessing Christian.' All this did not please Miriam. Miriam was shocked when it was decided that 'proper wedding at the cross' must be conducted. Miriam had already been married to Wariuki for several years and they had children. What was all this talk about another wedding merely for respectability, and as an excuse to expand excess income? But Miriam was persuaded, and she yielded. Wariuki wanted the early memory of this poverty erased for ever, and he selected the Church as the place to do that.

When it was time for the wedding ceremony, Miriam knew what to do. Her decision was shocking to her parents and her husband, but it was firm. When she was asked whether she would accept Wariuki to be her husband, as the formality requires, Miriam replied, 'No I cannot . . . I cannot marry Livingstone (Wariuki had already taken a more respectable name) . . . because . . . I have been married before. I am married to . . . Wariuki . . . and he is dead.'[53]

In Ngugi's implication, the Church as a structure contributed to Wariuki's death, by baptizing him into fashion and respectability.

In the third story, Ngugi takes another aspect of contemporary life, and exposes another shortcoming of the Church as a structure. Funerals are taken no longer as seriously as they used to be. They have become platforms to display wealth and respectability. A respectable person and his relatives and friends must be given a respectable burial, with beautiful eulogies at the funerals. The Church accepts responsibility to conduct such funerals. Why? Mainly, Ngugi suggests, for money.

Wahinya died of alcoholic poisoning during the campaigns for elections in his area. He was a watchman employed by one of the candidates, who was a parliamentarian. Though there had been no major policy issues in the campaign, Wahinya became an issue. One of the candidates had been campaigning claiming to be for the poor, while all others claimed that poverty was the result of laziness. When Wahinya died, the candidates began to fight among themselves as to who should bury him, because arrangements for the funeral would give the lucky candidate the coverage he needed for his campaign. Ngugi is concerned that death has come to mean very little because life has become less important than money. And the Church in Ngugi's view, in practice supports this situation, because it blesses those who claim to be Christians and to support such a situation.

In the words of the narrator of his story, *A Mercedes Funeral*, Ngugi observes:

> Now I don't know if it is true in your area, but in our village funerals had become a society affair, our version of cocktail parties. I mean since independence. Before 1952, you know, before the emergency, the body would be put away in puzzled silence and tears. People, you see, were awed by death. But they confronted it because they loved life. They asked: What's death? because they wanted to know what was life. They came to offer sympathy and solidarity to the living and helped in the burial. A pit. People took turns to dig it in ritual silence.[54]

Comparing this social concern for life death in traditional African Society, the narrator goes on to show what has happened in contemporary society.

> Shall we ever capture that genuine respect for death in an age where money is more important than life? Today what is left? A showbiz status. Even poor people will run into debts to have the death of a relative announced on the radio and funeral arrangements advertised in the newspapers. And gossip ... gossip. How many attended the funeral? How much money was collected? What of the coffin? Was the pit cemented? Plastic flowers: plastic tears. And evey year, there is an ad. (Advertisement) addressed to the dead.[55]

Wahinya's death was used as a campaign strategy. After reading the story one is left wondering whether the prominent candidate, who also offered his car for the funeral, may have organized the death! But the concern of this study for the story, is that Rev Bwana Solomon, was there to bless the funeral. The funeral attracted people of all religions and Christian denominations. It was conducted on a Sunday. Many came in buses and hired lorries.

Even the priest, Rev Bwana Solomon, who normally would not receive bodies of non-active members into the holy building unless of course they were rich and prominent, this time arrived early in resplendent dark robes laced with silver and gold. A truly memorable service, especially the beautiful trembling voice of Rev Solomon as he intoned:

> Blessed are the meek and poor for they shall inherit the earth ... (After the Church service the coffin was moved to the place of burial).
> After the prayers, Again Rev Solomon with his beautiful trembling voice captured many hearts, the amount of money each candidate had donated was announced.[56]

Ngugi's concern for the way in which the Church is responding to contemporary life, is clearly noticeable in these stories.

NOTES

1. Ngugi wa Thiong'o, *A Grain of Wheat*, London: Heinemann African Writers Series 36, 1967, p. 18. These are the words of Kihika, one of the characters in the novel.
2. Ngugi wa Thiong'o (James Ngugi) *Weep Not Child*, London: Heinemann African Writers Series 7, 1964. This was his first novel to be published.
3. *op. cit.* p. 35.
4. *op. cit.* pp. 34-35.
5. *op. cit.* p. 88.
6. *op. cit.* p. 59.
7. *op. cit.* pp. 87-88.
8. *op. cit.* pp. 143-144.
9. Hence the slogan *Gutiri Mubia na Muthungu*. (There is no difference between a white missionary and other categories of Europeans.) All are invaders, furthering their own interests. See Ngugi wa Thiong'o, *Home Coming*, London: Heinemann, 1972, p. 28; Okot p'Bitek, *African Religions in Western Scholarship*, Nairobi: East African Literature Bureau, 1970, p. 104.
10. Rosalind Mutua, *Development of Education in Kenya*, Nairobi: East African Literature Bureau, 1975, pp. 25-47, 56-58.
11. For example, the British National Anthem was translated into Kikuyu and published in the Anglican Hymn Book.
12. For a detailed study of the development of the Elite in Kenya, See B E Kipkorir, 'The Alliance High School and the Development of the Elite in Kenya,' Ph.D. Thesis, Cambridge University, 1970.
13. R Mutua, *op. cit.* pp. 30-31.
14. ibid.
15. Ngugi wa Thiong'o (James Ngugi) *The River Between*, London: Heinemann Africa Writers Series 17, 1965.
16. See Note 1 above.
17. R Mutua, *op. cit.* pp. 27-30.
18. Most missionaries believed that their task was to turn Africans from African culture into faithful imitation of their own. Dr. Clive Irvine, A Scottish Presbyterian Missionary, was the first European posted in 1922 to Chuka - Chogoria on the eastern slopes of Mount Kenya. To facilitate his mission of 'civilization,' he wrote a small book in English (out of print) entitled *How to Behave*. Other missionaries used the booklet as a manual for teaching their culture to Africans. On the missionaries'

understanding of their own task in Africa see, for example, R. Mcpherson, *The Presbyterian in Kenya*, Nairobi: PCEA, 1970; Anne King, 'J W Arthur and African Interest' in B E Kipkorir, ed., *Imperialist and Collaboration in Colonial Kenya: Biographical Essays*, Nairobi Literature Bureau, 1980, pp. 87-111; B E Kipkorir, Carley Francis at the Alliance High School, Kikuyu, 1940-62,' in B E Kipkorir, ed., *op. cit.* pp. 112-159.

19.   For example, the character of Isaka in *Weep Not Child,* Joshua in *The River Between*.

20.   ibid.

21.   op. cit. p. 21.

22.   op. cit. p. 36.

23.   ibid.

24.   ibid.

25.   R Mutua, *op. cit.* pp. 25-26, J A P Kiera, 'The Holy Ghost Fathers in East Africa 1863' Ph.D. Thesis, University of London, 1966.

26.   Micere Githae Mugo, unpublished poem, 'Don't be a Gabbage.'

27.   As far as I am aware, this is the first East African challenge of the authenticity of the sayings attributed to Jesus. It indicates the first signs that deep Biblical criticism may become a significant feature of future discussions about christianity in East Africa. *The River Between*, pp. 117, 154, *Weep Not, Child*, pp. 55-56, 61.106-107.

29.   *op. cit.* pp. 116-117.

30.   ibid.

31.   *op. cit.* p. 61.

32.   *op. cit.* p. 61.

33.   *The River Between*, pp. 117, 154.

34.   For a brief study of the E.A. Revival see George K. Mambo 'The Revival Fellowship in Kenya,' in *Kenya Churches Handbook*. Nairobi: Evangel Press, 1974, pp. 110-117

35.   George K Mambo, *op. cit.* See also the character of Jackson in *A Grain of Wheat*.

36.   *op. cit.* p. 97.

37.   Rosalind Mutua, *op. cit.* p. 25.

38.   For some details on how this testimony is conducted see Dorothy E Smoker, 'Decision Making in East African Revival Movement Groups' in D B Barrett (ed), *African Initiatives in Religion*, Nairobi: East African Publishing House, 1971, pp. 96-108.

39.   Bible studies are central to the Fellowship meeting. See Dorothy W E Smoker, *op. cit.* p. 96.

40.   See note 36 above.

41.   Henry Okullu, *Church and Politics in East Africa*, Nairobi: Uzima Press, 1974.

42.   *Weep Not, Child*, p. 115.

43.   *A Grain of Wheat*, pp. 98-99.

44.   ibid. p. 99.

45.   ibid. p. 99

46.   Ngugi wa Thiong'o, *Secret Lives*, London: Heinemann African Writers Series 150, 1975, p. 66.

47.   ibid. p. 7.

48.   ibid. Preface.

49.   ibid. pp. 84-85

50.   ibid. p. 94.

51.   ibid. p. 98.
52.   ibid. p. 100.
53.   ibid. p. 112.
54.   ibid. p. 118.
55.   ibid. p. 118.
56.   ibid. pp. 133-34.

Chapter Eight

TABAN LO LIYONG

I create on paper
And regard myself
A God and believe in myself
the best thing to do
Especially for those who believe in nothing.[1]

Taban Lo Liyong is another East African creative writer who has been critical of Christianity. Unlike Ngugi wa Thiong'o whose criticism of Christianity is based on his observations of the established and structured collaboration between colonial powers and the missionary societies, especially in Central Kenya, Taban Lo Liyong's criticism is based on his scepticism with regard to religion in general. He thinks that religion is a drawback, a hindrance to human intellectual and cultural development, and should, therefore, be attacked and abandoned, in order to set the human genius free. Belief in a god or gods, for Taban, is a short-cut which humankind has devised in order to avoid confronting the reality of his situation. Humankind has failed to establish courage in itself by inventing religion, and transferring all the potential which would otherwise be used to improve the material and intellectual conditions, to the beliefs in a god or gods:

Confidence in ourselves
Makes us responsible
For our own actions
Since the World's Gods and Satans
Are conveniences for shifting blame
Or covering modesty—
In short, Scapegoats.[2]

This view applies to the beliefs in gods in all religions, including those in the African heritage. Taban thinks that Africans must not be reduced to objects of study distinct from all the rest of humankind. For this reason he is very critical of the negritude school of African intellectuals because negritudism tended to exalt the blackness of the African as a quality which symbolized the uniqueness of the African race in the context of universal humanity. As far as Taban is concerned, the era of negritude has passed and served its purpose in the history of Africa. African intellectuals now ought to concentrate on more positive and constructive reflections about the role of the African individuals and African societies, first for themselves in Africa, and secondly as members of a universal international community.[3]

With regard to negritude, Taban considers those East Afrcans who advocate the reinstatement of African dignity through a revival of the traditional African customs, as neo-negritudists who must be attacked and opposed through intellectual debate. One of those whom he criticises in this respect, is Okot p'Bitek.[4] Taban complains that Okot is sympathetic to Lawino in his long poem, *Song of Lawino*.[5] Lawino, the illiterate woman who is abandoned by her husband Ocol after Ocol has gone through European book-learning and acculturation, laments the cultural death of her husband. She mourns for her 'dead' who is physically alive, but culturally lost in the strange ways of the colonial master. At the same time, Ocol takes up a concubine who is a town woman, a prostitute who spends her time and money in stinking bars and night-clubs. Ocol, having imbibed the new education, thinks that a 'civilized' person should not associate himself with rural uncivilized, illiterate and old fashioned women. So he feels comfortable in the night-clubs, with his 'sucker' Clementine. As far as Lawino is concerned, Ocol is lost, and shaken, because he has abandoned the customs of his people, and left his wife.

Symbolically, Okot has selected the pumpkin, a staple crop of the Acholi of Uganda, about whom he writes. Ocol is accused by his wife, Lawino, of uprooting the pumpkin in the old homestead. The accusation comes because of Ocol's decision to make a radical break from his own cultural and religious heritage, into a foreign way of life in which he imitates but never becomes a full participant. Lawino also complains about the woman whom Ocol has selected to become his new partner. She complains because Clementine has distorted the traditional African concept of beauty, and abused it, by burning her hair, painting her lips with lipstick, and colouring her skin pink in an attempt to look like European women.[6]

While Okot is sympathetic with Lawino, Taban's sympathy goes to Ocol. Taban's style makes his readers get the impression that Taban himself fits the character of Ocol. The attitude which Ocol has, and which Okot attacks, is the very attitude which Taban praises, and opts for, with the important difference that Ocol upholds the outward norms of 'Western Christianity, such as names, crosses, attending Church worship, and looking down upon African religious heritage. For Taban all religious traditions must be shattered in order to set humanity free from the wrath of the gods and satans who have been created by men, for the service of humanity, only to become tyrants later.

> You know we created him, God I mean,
> And therefore we can kill him.
> And that is what I am proceeding to do.
> Unfortunately, when I am done with hitting him,
> I might discover I was beating a dead horse.
> For had Nietsche not proclaimed: God is dead?
> The death of an idea, unfortunately, takes a long time,
> Like conspirators singing a tedious antiphony,
> Or frogs by the stream
> Who cease their croaking
> When they hear your footsteps
> But resume their disturbances.
> When your back is turned,
> Or like night darkness
> Which pushes the car impatiently on
> Angry at the disturbances
> Caused by the headlights.[7]

Taban thinks that God is an idea invented by human beings. The project of killing God, a task on which he has embarked, is going to take long to complete, because ideas take a long time to fade from people's memories. For him, however, the death of God is a matter of education and time. As a creative writer, he believes that he has a major role, to teach culture and to teach wisdom. That, for Taban, is the function of literature. With regard to Christianity, Taban would follow his project by destroying the basis of religions first, and then emphasizing the irrelevance of Christianity as one of the religions of mankind.[8]

In one of his later publications Taban has made a definite statement about religion and politics in contemporary Africa. In *Thirteen Offensives Against Our Enemies*, (1973), Taban reiterates the view he mainted eight years before when he published *The Last Word*, that there is no need for Africans to continue shouting about Africanness while the fact remains that there are no pure Africans without influence from European and Asian races.[9]

Taban recognizes that Christianity has already become established in Africa, and does not wish it out of the continent. He recognizes also that Islam is established in Africa, and does not seem likely to be cast out of the continent. The main question which he tries to answer here, is what he should say about the suggestion of 'making religion a pillar of politics in Africa.' Aware of what some African intellectuals have been recommending with regard to this issue, Taban notes that one suggestion is for Africans to abandon all foreign religions, and stick to their own heritage. But Taban has difficulty with this recommendation, because Africa has already been influenced by externl factors from East and West. He, therefore, rejects such an answer. He suspends an immediate solution, and places his hope in the future. For the present, Africans should experiment as much as possible, and imbibe as much of foreign culture as possible.[10] Taban accepts the supremacy of the West in all aspects, as a given fact. He suggests that Africans have to be willing to acknowledge this supremacy, and learn from the West.[11] For him, colonialism and the missionary enterprise are facts of history, and should be put in the archives where they belong. They should not be used daily to justify the 'laziness' and inability of Africans to control their own affairs.[12]

Taban recognizes also the fact that the Christian denominations are tied historically to their countries of origin, just as Islam is tied historically to the Arabic countries. For Africa, Taban warns against political alliance with any of these, because of the repercussions of such an alliance. Africans can no longer collaborate with the Churches in the same way as the missionary societies collaborated with the missionary societies.

> Now, about your proposal to make religion a pillar of politics in Africa, I have this to say. Which religion shall we use? For Christianity is already here—very firmly rooted and in places better rooted than in England and America. For Islam too is very committed and the modern countries have definitely made it a state religion; For with Christianity, there are two main branches: Catholicism and Protestantism and one comes from the Pope in Rome and the other the Queen in England, so how can one convert Catholicism into a religion without bringing Papal interference? So how can Protestantism be made a state religion without Anglican egoism and Catholic indignation? And how can Islam be made a state religion without giving undue honour and economy to Mecca and change the resting day?[13]

Those Africans who might want to re-educate the African society back to the traditional heritage, are also warned by Taban. The exercise will be a failure, in Taban's view, and an adoption of the same method which the Christian missionaries used. To re-convert Africans back into their pre-colonial religious beliefs is to put back the clock of history, and it is also to commit the error which the missionaries fell in when they brainwashed Africans to forget or abandon their heritage, and after cleaning up the 'blackboard of faith,' the missionaries poured in the newly imported doctrines. Those Africans who recommend the re-establishment of a purely African religion, are contradicting themselves when they condemn the missionaries, because re-conversion of Africans will involve another brainwashing. Such a programme does not win the favour of Taban.

But you had said . . . we should look for a religion thoroughly African. About that I have this reply to give: When did Africa in Africa end and non-Africa in Africa began?

For dress cloth(e) the flesh and bones and frame and they are constantly in fashion . . . . Furthermore, I know for a fact that the missionaries went about the problems of conversions the way you are re-discovering. So in order to create optimum condition for conversion they had to clean the blackboard of faith. And unbelievers we were all made before the tune was changed and belief was to be repoured-down our throat. But ah! Some of us unbrainwashed remarked the language sounds the same, the message hasn't changed at all, though the symbols are new.

And, now do we know this is the last change for, to be told to run very fast in a circle at night certainly makes no wonder in the morning when we find that we are not far away from the starting point.[14]

Concluding his reply, Taban has written:

Whether the grandmother is debrided in Christianity, or Islam or Atheism, or not is never an experiment to be tested. I would rather my grandmother lived a hundred and ten shielded from chaos she can't understand, leave alone resolve, rather than torment herself in doubt for my ideological pleasure: We conscripted tortures.[15]

In every case, Taban's conclusion is the same: do away with all religion, Christianity, Islam, African heritage—do away with all of them. Believe and re-establish confidence in yourself. Then look forward to the future to unfold itself.

What are the implications of implementing Taban's proposal? Taban is against any social norms which make demands on the individual, to conform. 'Normalcy, Normalcy I detest Thee!' That is what Taban maintains, because it forces people to become uniform following the norms which are dictated by others. Religion is often used as the seal to justify, authorize and legitimize these norms. Those that by nature have a different personality, are declared mad, and psychiatrists get jobs to do. 'I'd rather die a problem child than lie in the lamb on a psychiatric couch,' says Taban.

Obedience to a god, or gods, brings suffering, Taban thinks. In different parts of his writings, Taban repeats that 'Those whom the gods love, die young.' He gives the example of Abel who, though loved by God, was killed by his brother Cain. Taban interprets this to mean that it was not Cain who killed Abel, but rather it was Abel's obedience to God that led to his death. Cain is excused by Taban.[16]

Taban believes that the use of gods by religious leaders has led to too much suffering in the contemporary world, through the popularization of the doctrine that conformity is a virtue.

> Those whom the gods love die young;
> And whom man loves are killed by pills
> In the wombs of the mothers,
> Or smothered in the jackets of their fathers.
>
> We who escape infant mortality,
> Why not keep fertility
> Of the Mind alive?
> And replenish the fire
> (That Prometheus so kindly brought)
>
> Normalcy, normalcy, normalcy,
> I detest thee.
> Borne of the Joneses who mean well;
> The priests of Old and juju witches;
> The advertising men;
> Or the modern psychiatrists
> I detest thee, normalcy.[17]

In defense of this view, Taban was involved in a heated debate in 1973, over the popularity of the novel by Charles Mangua, *Son of Woman*.[18] To many East Africans, especially Christians, missionaries and other foreigners, this book was not fit for the East African reading public. The book became so popular that it was read in every class of the East African literate society. It was read by school children, bus conductors, cooks, hotel waiters, bar-maids, secretaries, prostitutes—and even by university and college students. Within less than a year, it needed to be reprinted. Those who opposed the circulation of the book argued that it was pornographic—immoral and erotic. In a heated debate between Taban Lo Liyong and James Stewart in a meeting of intellectuals at the Goethe Institute in Nairobi, Taban asked Stewart:

> 'Who are you to come and tell ten thousand East Africans that they are wrong? Do you buy the book for them, or do they use your eyes to read *Son of Woman?*[19]'

The novel, *Son of Woman,* is about the son who was born in a brothel area in Nairobi and became a drop-out in society even before he was born. Being the son of a prostitute, a bastard, he could not be socially accepted in respectable society. In spite of his university education at Makerere, Dodge Kiunyu was a drop-out in society. He did every thing wrong, according to the norms established in society.

Owing to the attitude which the society had on Kiunyu, and his society, Kiunyu, in order to survive, developed an attitude in which nothing seriously mattered in his life, except living for the moment, and living happily. Spontaneity was his motto, and planning his life was out of question. In this way he was able to survive, because the society came to accept him for what he was.

The priest at the mission station did not forgive him and welcome him genuinely as a person, as Kiunyu. He would have liked Kiunyu to change his personality and conform, before being accepted. But Kiunyu was not for that kind of demand. So the mission gave Kiunyu up, and Kiunyu knew how to take care of himself.

It seems that implicitly, Charles Mangua is challenging the rigid moral conformity which has led to hypocrisy in contemporary society. Kiunyu represents one of the consequences of this moral rigidity which Christianity has maintained in East Africa—in Africa as a whole. Kiunyu became what he was not because he was careless or immoral, but as a result of the society in which he grew. The Church ought to take responsibility for what it has produced in the character of Kiunyu. This is what Mangua seems to be saying in his two novels, Son of Woman and A Tail in the Mouth. [20] The books are popular, partly because they are written in the idiom which is in current use, especially in the towns, and partly because they deal with subjects which are relevant and deep in the contemporary society. In Son of Woman, Kiunyu ends up with a girl who, having been born in a brothel, herself became a prostitute, and after committing several abortions, destroyed all her possibilities of having any children. And what is an African woman without children? So she contemplated going to a convent, to become a nun, because that would be her only refuge, since nuns are not expected to have any children. Thus the novel challenges, in a light and readable way, though rather irritating to Christians, the contemporary norms which Christianity reinforces.

Mangua's attack on Christianity is similar to that of Ngugi in his short stories. It is on the Church as a structure which seems to condone hypocrisy and misuse of religion for personal and material self-aggrandisement. However, instead of behaving like Wariuki who wanted to 'ape' the norms established by the settler community, Dodge Kiunyu chose to be free, and to live according to the whims dictated by the circumstances in which he found himself.

The protest against Son of Woman was very strong among some missionaries, and the novel was proscribed in some secondary schools and colleges in Kenya. However, the proscription of such books only increases the curiosity of the people, who, somehow, find their own secret moments to read the books, be it at home or in school. A similar protest was also levelled against Mission to Kala by Mongo Beti, the Camerounian writer, on the ground that it was immoral. It is this kind of attitude that Taban challenges in religion. David Maillu's books have also faced similar accusations.

Taban, however, commended Mangua for exploring new forms of literary expression to expose the contemporary East African society. This kind of adventurism is what Taban cherishes. He likes Kiunyu for his sponteneity and readiness to live through any situation when it finds him, or when he finds it. In his comment about religion in *Thirteen Offensives Against Our Enemies*, Taban concludes:

> I am saying those (Africans) who are misusing religion now, or asking for its nationalization are heirs to the colonial mentality spelling *Abuse, appropriation,* etc.
>
> And the rest of us are justified in pilloring the scion plus his mentor,
> And therefore you are worse than the white man
> And can't ask him to defend you since you never forgave him but drove him out.
> And therefore our Salvation is still in the future. To be born of depth, understanding, patience, and heartache.[21]

As for the role of Christianity in Taban's vision of the future, he sees no role. All religion is unnecessary in his vision. He is definite in this position. According to him, 'Social prophets of our time need not go to Church.' But if this is true, then what is the role of the Church? Taban in his writings has repeated that the Church, and all religion in general, is a handicap preventing prophetic voices of our time from proclaiming their visions of a New Earth and a New Heaven. Both the missionaries and their African followers on one hand, and the advocates of African heritage on the other, are all guilty of hindering social and intellectual liberty, in Taban's opinion.[22]

NOTES

1. Taban Lo Liyong, *Frantz Fanon's Uneven Ribs Poems More and More*, London, Heinemann African Writers Series 90, 1971, p. 42.
2. ibid. p. 43.
3. ibid. pp. 120-126.
4. ibid. p. 126, *The Last Word*, pp. 135-156.
5. *The Last Word*, pp. 135-156.
6. Okot p'Bitek, *Song of Lawino* and *Song of Ocol*, Nairobi: East African Publishing House, 1966 and 1967, pp. 41-48.
7. *Frantz Fanon Uneven Ribs*, p. 44.

8. ibid
9. *The Last Word*, pp. 79, 187-210, *Thirteen Offensives Against Our Enemies*, pp. 6-20.
10. *Thirteen Offensives*, p. 20.
11. ibid.
12. ibid. pp. 39-40.
13. ibid p. 37.
14. ibid pp. 37-38.
15. ibid pp. 38-39.
16. Taban Lo Liyong, *Another Nigger Dead*, London, Heinemann African Writers Series.
17. *Frantz Fanon's Uneven Ribs*, p. 34.
18. Charles Mangua, *Son of Woman*, Nairobi: East African Publishing House, 1970.
19. Goethe Institute, 1971.
20. Charles Mangua, *A Tail in the Mouth*, Nairobi: East African Publishing House, 1973.
21. Taban, *Thirteen Offensives*, p. 40.
22. ibid.

Chapter Nine

KABIRU KINYANJUI

If the past has been unjust, will the future be equally so? The hopes of many
people is that tomorrow will be a better day if not for them, at least for their
children. As this process of questioning what development means to the
majority of Kenyans continues, the Church will be asked for guidance on
this important question, and at the same time, it will be required to sustain
many with its gospel of love and hope. It is imperative, therefore, that the
Church in this country should start serious discussions on what development means and consequently what social justice means to the majority of
our people.[1]

Kabiru Kinyanjui is concerned mainly with development. In an address to
the staff of the National Christian Council of Kenya in 1975, he challenged the
Church as a social structure to analyse the meaning of development, in its
contemporary and future contexts, and to order its involvement in the interests of
social justice for the majority of the people.[2] Kabiru does not discuss Christianity
from the doctrinal and theological perspectives. Rather, he concentrates on the
social structure on which Christian doctrines and theological positions have been
developed—structures which have become crucial factors in directing education
and development.[3] At a pastor's consultation in November, 1975, he made an
analysis of the structures of injustice and their effects on development, and in that
analysis he included the Church as one such structure.[4]

Kabiru does not end his criticism of the Church at the time when African
countries attained constitutional independence. Colonial history for him is to be
studied not merely to expose the failures of the imperial powers or to expose the
weaknesses of Africans who were subjugated. Rather, an analysis of social structures of

the colonial period will help to show the transition that came at the attainment of constitutional independence, and the relationship between the colonial structures and those that followed the constitutional independence of African countries. Kabiru's conclusion is that the new situation did not breed new social structures, and that in terms of development, the social structures were very closely related to those maintained by the colonial powers. Neo-colonialism was the result.[5]

For example, the role of the multinational corporations in contemporary Africa, has been to maintain and maximize the trading interests of leading business houses in the countries which formerly ruled Africa, and their allies.[6] With regard to the Churches, the Africanization of personnel has not led to a radical change of the executive and administrative procedures in those churches which were formerly controlled by the missionary societies, and boards.[7] Patterns of Church discipline which were established during the colonial period have not been radically changed, although the Churches controlled by foreign missions in the colonial period tended to be biased against Africans, and in favour of those who held colonial power.[8] Having noted that the main Churches of the colonial period were social establishments which aided the colonial administration to exploit Africans and keep them poor, Kabiru goes on to argue that the Church in contemporary East Africa, particularly in Kenya, has not got out of that position yet. It has continued to be one of the structures of injustice.[9]

Kabiru does not overlook the fact that the main Churches in colonial Africa were involved in giving aid to African communities. Neither does he ignore the efforts of the Churches in contemporary East Africa to participate in development. Nevertheless, one of his main criticism of the Church as a social structure, is that its attitude towards human development, has been that of charity, rather than helping Africans to help themselves: The same criticism has been made by Asian theologians on the Christian Missionary enterprise in Asia.[10]

> We must accept that what our people
> need is not charity but their own
> development.[11]

With these words, Kabiru recommends a new orientation. By contributing to Africa's development, on the basis of charity, Kabiru argues, the Churches have contributed to the establishment and maintenance of injustice. Recognizing the presence of the Church as a significant factor influencing the trend of development in contemporary Kenya, Kabiru challenges its leaders to provide the kind of guidance which will help Christians and the entire community to realize social justice, whose fruits will be manifested by equitable distribution of means of production, and the products of human labour to meet the basic needs of the majority.[12]

During a luncheon address to the National Christian Council of Kenya, Kabiru Kinyanjui observed that the Church throughout its history has been living in contradictions. On the one hand, the teachings of the Church have tended to be in sympathy with the poor and the oppressed. On the other hand, the Church structure has identified itself with the few who are wealthy and with those who oppress. This has been the case at least since the reign of Constantine, when Christianity became the fashionable religion of the Roman Empire. In spite of the poverty and the oppression which prevailed during the peaks of the empire, that empire was described as 'holy,' with the co-operation and blessing of the Church.[13] The same pattern was repeated after the Reformation. The Lutheran Church in Germany, founded by Martin Luther the renowned reformer, has been one of the most vehement opposers of the Programme to Combat Racism of the World Council of Churches.[14] The British Empire, at the time when, in theory, its administrators considered themselves most successful in propagating Christianity and civilization, was in practice most successful in oppressing and exploiting those whom it colonized. All this was done in the name of 'pacification' and the establishment of Law and Order, and 'legitimate trade.'[15] The propagation of 'commerce and Christianity' led not to the exultation of the dignity of African humanity, but rather, to the degradation of it.[16]

The presence and maintenance of Portuguese colonial rule in Africa was justified for five centuries as a responsibility heeded to Christianize and 'civilize' Africans.[17] When these and other examples are considered seriously, Kabiru's observation of the contradiction between Church-doctrine and Church-practice, has to be taken seriously. The Church teaches that its followers should follow the example of its founder Jesus Christ.[18] Yet the administrative structure of that Church tends not to facilitate such a possibility. In the Kenya press there was a discussion about the Anglican Archbishop of Canterbury who turned down an economy-class air ticket in order to fly first-class to attend the World Council of

Churches Fifth Assembly in Nairobi. Archbishop Coggan was criticized for spending more than sixty pounds sterling extravagantly at a time when many people in the World, even within the Anglican Community, did not have adequate food shelter, medical care, and other basic necessities. This criticism is indicative of the contradiction which Kabiru exposes. The fact that this behaviour was highlighted by the Kenya press and discussed, is indicative of another disclosure, that Kabiru's point is not based on an isolated observation. He is not alone in his conclusion.[19]

Kabiru's challenge that the social involvement of the Church should shift from charity tokens, is similar to John Gatu's call for a moratorium on foreign Church funds and personnel. John Gatu, in his call for a moratorium, is *not* merely suggesting that African and Asian Christians should dissociate themselves from their fellowship with Christians in other parts of the contemporary world. Rather, the argument underlying the proposition of a moratorium, is that the Churches which have been under the control of foreign missionaries, have been unable to realize their selfhood even after substantial Africanization of personnel, and one of the main factors leading to this situation has been the presence of foreign funds and personnel, which have been donated but restricted by the donating Churches and missionary agencies in Europe, North America, and Australia. The decisions and plans of the 'established' Churches have been so greatly influenced by the missionary agencies which controlled those Churches during the colonial period, that the Churches have remained remarkably foreign social structures.[20]

At the same time, fellowship in the context of Christian theology implies a communion of committed Christians, equal before each other and before God. If foreign aid in terms of funds and personnel hinders the realization of meaningful fellowship, then this aid should be withdrawn as a positive step, not as a retrogressive one. In the secular and national plane, Kabiru observes that when the Church perpetuates structures which are against human development and social justice as he understands these concepts, then the Church has failed in its local mission.[21]

Although Kabiru is in apparent agreement with John Gatu and the advocates of Moratorium, he cautions that the Church should not identify itself too closely with the *status quo*, to the extent of involving governments in its fund-raising functions. This caution has also been made by Henry Okullu, as observed earlier in this study.[22] Therefore, financial self-reliance should not mean a shift from foreign missionary aid to a sort of government department aid financed through the government channels of power, influence or communication.

On this point, Kabiru Kinyanjui has warned that the Church must also be aware that involving government leaders in its fund-raising functions has its problems. One danger is that the politicians may tend to look upon the Church as another government department with the responsibility of saying prayers and preaching in favour of the government. This is something that must be avoided at all costs, because it can seriously compromise the Church's role in development. This is a challenge that the Church will need to face boldly.[23]

The critics of Moratorium base their argument mainly on the premise that this proposition implies cutting off Africans from the universal Christian community. This is a misunderstanding of the advocates of Moratorium, because the latter, by their proposal, indicate that the present situation, being dominated by those who have enough to meet their basic needs and to squander, have not been ensuring meaningful fellowship between African, Asian, European and American Christians.[24] Byang Kato, in *Theological Pitfalls in Africa*, used this as an argument against Moratorium. When the proposal of Moratorium was made, those who formulated it were aware of their reliance on foreign aid and personnel, and also of the fact that they could not bring abrupt changes in their Church structures without disrupting the social organization of their Churches. Therefore, the meaning of Moratorium has to be understood as having much deeper implications than merely cutting off the African Christian community from the rest of the Christians all over the world. Nor should Moratorium be interpreted as meaning the wholesale adoption of African culture into Christianity, as Kato suggests.[25] The call for African Christian Theology, is an expression of the felt need to articulate the Christian Faith in terms which are relevant and meaningful among Africans.

Kabiru Kinyanjui considers it necessary for the Church to be involved actively in bringing about development. According to his definition, development is not merely the acquisition and accumulation of material things such as money, roads, schools and the like. Nor should it be defined in terms of the rate of growth of the Gross National Product, or in terms of rising income per capita, industrialization, urbanization, bureaucratic efficiency and such concepts which are common in the categorization of the contemporary world into two, the developed countries and the developing countries. According to Kabiru Kinyanjui, in the last two development decades, many people have realized that the growth of GNP does not (necessarily) mean development. The people of third world countries who have seen the GNP of their countries rise while they sink into poverty are perhaps the people who can attest to the failure of the magic formula called economic growth. 'Economic growth . . . is only meaningful when the goods produced are vital to a majority of the people and are evenly distributed.'[26]

Kabiru rejects the prevalent notions of development, in which development is defined merely in terms of the rate of growth in Gross National Product and income per capita, industrialization, urbanization, bureaucratic efficiency, modernized political parties, and so on. Rather, he suggests that development is both a process and a state. This implies that it is a continuing process, while it can also refer to the historical stage of a particular society. Development represents an attempt by man to change his physical and social environment with the aim to make it better for human beings. 'The rate of this change differs from society to society . . . It involves total changes in economic, cultural, political and educational institutions and the values and beliefs that govern them. It implies a situation where people move from one level of human existence to a markedly higher quality of human life—where people have more freedom, human dignity and equality, and where they are active participants in the process that affects their lives, then we can say . . . there is development taking place.'[27]

Since the Church operates within society, it ought to be involved in the endeavour to bring about this form of qualitative change. Kabiru's proposal implies that a Church which fails to contribute towards development according to this concept of change, is irrelevant in terms of the crucial needs of that particular society. Though Kabiru does not state it, it seems that this concept of development is in accordance with the teaching of Jesus.[28] However, Kabiru does not base his convictions on Biblical reference. This is not his main concern. It seems that he leaves the Churches to define the theological basis for their social involvement. As far as his analysis is concerned, he does not see a need to bring the teaching of Jesus into the judgement of the social involvement of the Churches in a particular country or community. He is not a Christian and is, therefore, not obliged to discuss Jesus.[29]

It is important to remark that though Kabiru gives significant cautions about the failures of the Churches to be actively involved in effecting the positive transformation of society, there is evidence that some churches and church agencies have been involved in bringing about the kind of qualitative change which Kabiru supports. The National Christian Council of Kenya,[30] and the Kenya Catholic Secretariat[31] for example, have projects which help people to help themselves. The work of these organizations in Northern Kenya, in village polytechnics, in the development of cottage industries and in Mathare Valley slums of Nairobi, are illustrative of this kind of involvement. The Presbyterian Church of East Africa has a Rural Development Project among the Maasai which is based on this objective.[32]

At the same time, there are individual Christians who have expressed concern about the need for the kind of development which Kabiru argues for, and some of them have become actively involved in helping some helpless people to help themselves, going beyond the notion of charity which tends to perpetuate poverty.[33]

Kabiru indicates that, in his understanding, development is *not* through an exposition of common concepts. He then continues to provide a positive definition, and a set of criteria by which the level of development may be assessed in any particular country. The following is his concise statement of what development ought to mean to an individual, and also to a nation:

> To an individual, and indeed a nation, development means (ought to mean) realization of total humanity and personality. It means (ought to mean) liberation from all aspects of economic, spiritual, political and psychological forms of domination and exploitation. The struggle for liberation, the total development of man, is a continuing struggle . . . The Church in this country (Kenya) must stand for full development of all people.[34]

Although he is aware that not all people will accept his definition, Kabiru proceeds to indicate some of the criteria which may help to assess the level of development in a particular country, according to the definition he has proposed.

The first criterion is the level of poverty in the country.

> What is the level of poverty in this country? Our concern here is with basic necessities—food, clothing, shelter and footwear. Are people still hungry, unnourished, without vital proteins and without shelter? It is true these things can be expressed in terms of income, but we should be aware of what income can·buy and cannot buy. How is food distributed? How is housing distributed, especially in the urban areas?[35]

Again, Kabiru does not provide a straight-forward answer to these questions; he leaves it to those concerned to analyse their own situations and to realize the trend of development on the basis of the criteria he has provided.

Kabiru considers inequality as a second criterion for assessing the level of development. By inequality he refers to the income range between the people in the country, and also to the availability of opportunities and facilities which are necessary for the realization of fuller humanity and personal dignity. In this regard, he raises questions about the distribution of available arable land, especially that which during the colonial period the European colonists had set aside for themselves. He also asks what the Africanization of businesses through state corporations and banks has meant in terms of the distribution of wealth. Another question he asks is about the implications of the salary structure in terms of the relationship between the high scales and the low ones; between the incomes of urban communities and those of the rural communities.[36] Still, with regard to the problem of inequality, Kabiru asks what the existence of the two types of educational institutions—the Primary and Secondary school levels, —means in terms of unequal access to education and the perpetuation of inequalities within the society.[37]

The third criterion is concerned with independence. Kabiru asks whether total independence has been achieved:

> Is the country truly independent, economically, politically, culturally and pyschologically? Is the country still a dependency of another country? This question is crucial in the process of our development as continued economic and cultural aspects of dependency is (are) a real

hindrance to realization of liberation. We have to ask ourselves what implications institutions like tourism, education and the Church have in continuing psychological dependency.[38]

These three criteria for assessing the level of development help, in Kabiru's view, to indicate how much development has been achieved within a particular country or community. The criteria place emphasis on qualitative change among the members of the community under consideration, rather than on material acquisitions of that particular community. Kabiru does not ignore or overlook the necessity of material acquisitions, but he emphasizes that such acquisitions ought to be related to a qualitative change in the lives of those among whom such properties are found.

As far as the role of the Church in development is concerned, Kabiru suggests that it should be involved in helping the people among whom it witnesses, to realize social justice, by helping to raise the level of development according to his definition and on the basis of the criteria he has indicated. If the Church is genuinely interested in working for social justice, he argues, it should start working for equal distribution of income, resources like land, education and political power. It should be working for the transformation of the present society, so that the benefits of development can reach the mass of the people. For the Church to accept the present structure of the society with the inequalities that exist thereof, will be tantamount to acceptance of social injustice. This is a real challenge for the Church in this country (Kenya).'[39]

One of the concerns of Kabiru with regard to the Church in contemporary East Africa, arises from his observation that during the colonial period the Church tended to favour the colonists more than the subjects.[40] This contradictory situation has placed the Church in independent Africa in a rather embarrassing situation. Most of the academically educated East Africans have hesitated to point out this contradiction.[41] Nevertheless, the Churches have continued to grow in numbers, especially in the rural areas.[42] What does this mean with regard to the future of the Church? It seems that African Church leaders have to work hard to overcome the contradictions and embarrassments which they inherited from the missionaries of the colonial period. They have to reverse the role of the Church, so that it becomes a social force which works in the interests of the African society, helping African communities to help themselves.

The Independent Churches have the motivation to work for the welfare of their members but in most cases they lack the knowledge and skills which are necessary for them to cope with the demands of contemporary society. The ecumenical organizations may serve a useful purpose in providing these basic necessities to such Churches through training.[43]

Very few of the Independent Churches have joined the ecumenical organizations such as the National Christian Council of Kenya. Though there is no exhaustive survey to indicate why this is the case, it appears that most of them are ignorant of the facilities which such ecumenical agencies provide, and that some are too small and unstable to consider joining the ecumenical movement. At the same time, the procedure of application for membership may be one of the hindrances, because, in the case of the National Christian Council of Kenya, for example, an applying member is required to have sponsorship from a full member of the Council. The ecumenical organizations such as NCCK have to decide whether to limit services only to members.[44]

The question of Church co-operation is crucial to the total witness and involvement of the Church in development. The impact of joint Church programmes in a community may bring greater achievements in terms of the qualitative development which Kabiru supports, than projects which are organized on denominational and often competitive basis. The Church, as a social force in society, needs to overcome its internal strife, for the sake of national development. Until such co-operation is effected at the local community levels, both in the rural and urban areas, the Church will continue to receive heavy criticism from those who do not see its social relevance in national development.[45] Ecumenical efforts need to go beyond Church-union discussions, which seem never to achieve much.

In Kabiru's view, the Church is beset with a number of problems, which it must overcome in order to be effected in its social involvements for the realization of development and social justice.

The first of these problems is conservatism, especially with regard to the participation of its members in political, economic and social affairs. Emphasis on personal spiritual salvation has tended to be so strong a concern in many of the East African Churches, that the need for the converts to involve themselves in the total life of the society, has been neglected. Some Church leaders have categorically opposed the involvement of their followers in any endeavours for national development and social justice.[46] Byang Kato, for example, is critical of the World Council of Churches because of its programmes on development. His criticism of Philip Potter, General Secretary of the World Council of Churches, is typical of the criticisms on the attitude of those church leaders who feel that involvement in total development is not a priority for their followers. What Africa needs most, Kato has written, is the new life in Christ, and the power of the Holy Spirit which enables Christians to live for Christ in all aspects of life, justice included.[47]

Theologically, there may be nothing objectionable in this statement. However, there has been tendency among many conservative evangelicals to use their zeal for the Christian faith as an excuse for their passivity in matters related to social development. Jesus, it may be observed, was concerned with the welfare of the whole human being, and spiritual wholeness was only an aspect of his total ministry. To Kabiru's observation of the Church's conservatism with regard to practical involvement, may be added the fact that the Church has been generally conservative, theologically.[48]

In Kabiru's analysis, the second problem with which the Church should deal, is ignorance. He observes that the majority of Church members are not aware of what Church involvement in development means. The strength of the Church comes from these members and it is this strength which will make it a voice in the wilderness of our society. Unless, therefore, the members are fully conscious of what the Church and organizations like the NCCK stand for, their role will be considerably weakened. It is imperative, therefore, that the Church's leadership should take it upon itself to educate its members on all issues relating to development.[49]

Kabiru cautions that if this warning is not heeded, there is likely to be little or no support for Church programmes which are aimed at participation in development.

The third problem facing the Church is its relationship with the state. When the state guarantees and protects freedom of worship, the Churches may feel so indebted to the state that they may cease to raise the prophetic voice which is a necessary challenge in the endeavour for human development. In suggesting a solution to this problem, Kabiru advises that the Church must make it known clearly that the freedom of worship is a basic human right which must be protected by the government in power as it protects the lives of its citizens.[50]

This position is similar to that held by Henry Okullu, though Kabiru expresses his interpretation in different words.

The fourth problem facing the Church is concerned with leadership. Kabiru suggests that the prophetic challenge which the Church should place on the contemporary situation, will be silenced if the leadership of the Church indentifies itself with the oppressing and exploiting classes of the society to which the Church speaks and ministers.

The Church in the colonial period accepted colonialism as a system and operated within it without condemning it as an evil system. 'The Church in Kenya must be made aware of implications of its leadership becoming part of the national bourgeoisie.'[51]

Kabiru seems to suggest that the leaders of the Church in Kenya ought not to become land owners, businessmen and landlords. They ought not to accept the ideology of private ownership, because if they accept these things it will be extremely difficult for the Church to question that system.

Kabiru does not declare explicitly how he thinks Church leaders should conduct themselves with regard to practical life within prevailing social, economic and political policies. However, he makes his point clear, that if the leadership of the Church indentifies its interests with those of the privileged and exploiting minority, then it will be very difficult for such leadership to speak for the oppressed, the exploited, and the powerless, as Jesus proclaimed He had come to do.

NOTES

1. Kabiru Kinyanjui, 'Development, Social Justice and Church,' A paper given at the national Christian Council of Kenya Staff Consultation of Limuru, 6 February, 1975, p. 1.
2. ibid. p. 1.
3. Interview, 22 December, 1975.
4. The consultation was organized by the NCCK on Structures of Injustice and Struggles for Liberation, in preparation for WCC 5th Assembly. The Report was compiled by the Department of Church, Industry and Commerce, NCCK.
5. Interview, 22 December, 1975, NCCK Pastors' Consultation on Structures of Injustice and Struggles for Liberation, See Note 4 above.
6. B N Y Vaughan, *The Expectation of the Poor: The Church and the Third World*, London: SCM Press, 1972, pp. 67-68, Also, Ruth First, *The Barrel of a Gun*, Penguin Press, 1970, *passim*.
7. Interview with Kabiru Kinyanjui, 22 December, 1975. In a Luncheon Forum organized by NCCK, Micere Mugo expressed her opinion that the Africanization of Church personnel will not automatically lead to a radical change in Church organization, unless the Africans who take over are willing to change. John Gatu expressed the same feeling in another Forum in January, 1976.
8. The issue of marriage and ordination of women may be taken as examples here. See Adrian Hastings, *Christian Marriage in Africa*, London: SPCK, 1973. This book is the publication of a Report commissioned by the Anglican Archbishops of Cape Town, Central Africa, Kenya, Tanzania and Uganda.
9. Interview, 22 December, 1975. See also Note 4 above.
10. The criticism is repeated in the Christian Conference of Asia Newsletter, January, 1976.
11. Kabiru, 'Development, Social Justice and the Church' p. 5.
12. Kabiru did not bring Karl Marx into this discussion, and the realization of justice for the majority of people through dialectical class struggle, did not form part of his presentation. However, he emphasized that if the Church wants to struggle for justice, then it must try to help the majority to realize that ideal.
13. It is difficult to cite a single volume which would cover all European History in depth. For a brief study of this point, see H A L Fisher, A *History of Europe, Volume 1, From the Earliest Times to 1713*, London: Collins Fontana Library, 1935.
14. Elizabeth Adler, *A Small Beginning: An Assessment of the First Five Years of the Programme to Combat Racism*. Geneva: WCC Publication, 1974, pp. 65-66.

15. S Kiwanuka, *From Colonialism to Independence*, Nairobi: East African Literature Bureau, 1973 *passim*. Also, E S Atieno Odhiambo, *The Paradox of Collaboration and Other Essays,* Nairobi: East African Literature Bureau, 1974, p. 122.

16. See, for example, the essays written by South Africans and Published — Theo Sundermeier, (ed.), *Church and Nationalism in South Africa,* Johannesburgh: Ravan Press, 1975. Also M S M Kiwanuka, 'Uganda Under the British' in B A Ogot and J Kieran (eds.), *Zamani,* Nairobi: East African Publishing House and Longman Kenya, 1969, p. 323.

17. The same argument was used by Carl McIntire to justify the Smith Minority Regime, during the 9th Congress of the International Council of Christian Churches, Nairobi, 18-25 July 1975. Micere Githae Mugo heavily criticized McIntire for his view; McIntire was deported from Kenya before the end of the Meeting. See the reports of Kenya Daily papers of the relevant period.

18. *Redemption Songs*, London: Pickering and Inglis, nd., No. 50.

19. See, for example, *Target*, 23 November 1975, p. 1.

20. For example, in Administration, Liturgy, Hymns, Architecture, "Theology, Vestments.

21. Kabiru, *op. cit.* p. 8.

22. ibid. p. 7. cf. Henry Okullu, *Church and Politics in East Africa*, pp. 17, 28. See also ch. 7 above.

23. Kabiru, *op. cit.* pp. 7-8.

24. For the pros and cons of the Moratorium Debate see Elliot Kendall, *The End of an Era*: *Africa and the Missionary*, London: SPCK, 1978.

25. Byang Kato, *Theological Pitfalls in Africa*, Kisumu, Kenya: Evangel, 1975, pp. 166-167.

26. Kabiru, *op. cit.* pp. 2-3.

27. ibid. p. 3.

28. Luke, 4: 16-18.

29. Interview with Kabiru Kinyanjui, 22 December, 1975.

30. See Annual Reports of NCCK, Nairobi.

31. See Department Reports, Catholic Secretariat, Nairobi.

32. During the WCC 5th Assembly the PCEA staged a stand at Kenyatta Conference Centre, showing some of the crafts produced at their centres. The Isinya Rural Development Centre (Maasailand) is about sixty kilometres from Nairobi.

33. For example, the (car) parking boys in Nairobi are receiving help from committed individual Christians. Father Arnold Grol has committed his efforts to helping these boys to help themselves — Mathare Valley, Nairobi.

34. Kabiru, *op. cit.* p. 3.

35. ibid. p. 4.

36. ibid., p. 4.

37.   ibid. p. 4.
38.   ibid. p. 4.
39.   ibid. p. 5.
40.   Interview, 22 December, 1975. Also, E S Atieno Odhiambo, *op. cit.* p. 22.
41.   For example, Ngugi wa Thiong'o, Okot, p'Bitek, Micere Githae Mugo, M S M Kiwanuka, . . . the list is long. The views of many of these people are cited in this study.
42.   This is shown in *Kenya Churches Handbook,* Kisumu: Evangel Press, 1973. Also, D B Barett, *Schism and Renewal in Africa,* Oxford, 1968.
43.   The degree of literacy tends to be lower in the Independent Churches than in the 'Established' ones, to the extent that some of the leaders of Independent Churches are non-literate. The ecumenical Church organizations may find it difficult to design projects which would be fruitful to such illiterate Church Members.
44.   Though the projects of NCCK have not been restricted to member Churches, it may raise difficulties if programmes were started for the sake of a Church or Churches which did not belong to the organization. Projects of the NCCK serve the needy, irrespective of denominational affiliation.
45.   Kabiru, an interview, 22 December, 1975.
46.   Kabiru, *op. cit.* p. 7
47.   Byang Kato, *op. cit.* p. 166.
48.   Conservation helps the Church to maintain a continuous link between past, present and future. Kabiru, *op. cit.* p. 7.
49.   There are signs that this re-education has begun; Henry Okullu's *Church and Politics in East Africa* serves that purpose. There are frequent pastors' consultations organized by the NCCK. See also *Gospel and Revolution,* a booklet which was circulated among church leaders in Tanzania as a Christian Message, 1973.
50.   Kabiru, *op. cit.* p. 7. He stresses this point in order to caution the churches against being used by politicians as platforms for the manoeuvre and manipulation of Christians through the offer of the freedom of worship. cf. Henry Okullu, *Church and Politics in East Africa,* pp. 12-20.
51.   Kabiru, *op. cit.* p. 8. cf. Ngugi wa Thiong'o, *Homecoming.* London: Heinemann, 1972, pp. 31-38.
       pp. 31-38.

Chapter Ten

ODHIAMBO OKITE

My tribe says, 'When you look into the water, from above you see only the reflection of your face; when you see under the water, you see clearly what is in the lake and what is above it as well.' Originally, the saying was directed to the fishermen who in the old days, used spears to fish in Lake Victoria. They would go under, so to speak, to gain perspective. Today, the saying is a favourite with preachers who use it to illustrate the great truths of the Gospel, from the incarnation of Christ to the essence of the Christian mission in the world.[1]

Odhiambo Okite has reflected on the situation of Christianity not only in contemporary East Africa, but also in North America in October and November 1974 with a 'Mission ... to try to persuade a few North Americans to share with us ... what they hear through their third year.' During his visit he interviewed many North Americans in the United States and in Canada, and his questions were aimed at discovering what the Christians in that part of the world think of their faith. The answers he received were not very encouraging, and led him to the following conclusions:

The Continent (North America) is experiencing a profound cultural and spiritual crisis, structures and attitudes that took centuries to form are discarded as people seek new ideas, a new spirituality, and new life-styles. Some of the voices interpreting the scene are uncertain as to the value and viability of the experiments; those who seem certain contradict one another at crucial points. And those who believe in a living God who is active in human history are aware that somehow in all this, God is acting and speaking.[2]

Does this conclusion also apply in the East African situation? Okite notes some similarities between contemporary Africa and North America, but also some remarkable differences. In both continents there is a rapid multiplication of Christian denominations, and in both areas the denominations and sects have tended to be very parochial and self-centred.

In Africa as well as in North America, denominational division has run rampant, and in both places the sects and denominations have tended to reflect strongly the local culture.[3]

In Africa, David Barrett made a study of more than six thousand Independent Churches in 1968, and this number is likely to have risen considerably since that time. His publication of *Schism and Renewal in Africa* revealed, with facts, that there is a widespread dissatisfaction among African Christians with the brands of Christianity which had been introduced to Africa through the Missionary enterprise.[4] Both David Barrett and Odhiambo Okite suggest that the Independent Churches need to be taken seriously, because, they are attempts to renew, reform or break away from the 'mother Churches' in order to participate fully in a more relevant and meaningful expression of their Christian faith.

However, Okite has noted a significance difference between the situations in Africa and in North America. In the latter situation, the Christian sects were started within a context where Christianity was taken for granted by the ruling classes. The Europeans who went to settle in North America were mainly Christians who could not tolerate the norms set by the established Church in Europe, and sailed to North America in search of freedom. There they established a way of life which was loosely described as Christian, and which became the foundation of the respectable standards of American citizenry. Such is the background from which American sects have developed. It is a nominally Christian background; in which the majority claim to be Christian although in practice this nominal claim is not backed by a corresponding conduct.[5]

The multiplication of Christian denominations in contemporary Africa has developed from a different background. Africa, with the exception of Ethiopia and Egypt, does not have a long Christian tradition. The effective introduction of Christianity in most of Africa has taken place within the last two centuries, long after the Reformation in Europe. Some students of the history of Christian missions have interpreted the expansion of Christianity from Europe to Africa as one of the by-products of the Reformation. Whereas Christianity was planted in Africa through the missionary enterprise, it was established in North America by emigrants who were running away from their home countries in search of religious and other forms of freedom.

David Barrett's study shows that the mulitiplication of Christian denominations in contemporary Africa is mainly due to the growing numbers of Independent Churches.[6] Most of those Churches have been founded during the twentieth century, and are part of the expression of the resistance against the cultural and religious imperialism of the Western World. However, Okite has observed that Christianity is expanding in contemporary Africa during the era of ecumenism and international co-operation, at a time when national isolation is no longer possible.

Africa, according to Okite, is more fortunate than North America. We (Africans) are receiving the Gospel in an ecumenical era in which the enemies of mankind on this small planet are an inescapable fact. We can avoid the absurdities of provincialism and of a cultural religion. Living outside any Christendom, we ought to be able to see the burden of our mission in the world, which is far more important than things that would divide the Christian community within a 'Christendom.'[7]

Okite, in his comparison of situations in Africa and North America, has observed that in the latter the assumed nominal commitment to Christianity led to a loose 'Christendom' in which Christianity was subordinated to the service of the nation, especially in the United States of America. Being an American became more important than being a Christian, to such an extent that the nation became a kind of God, and the American way of life became a kind of religion. This development is described by Okite as the 'civilizing' of religion.

> Americans may have gone too far in "civilizing" religion and making it serve largely secular and temporal ends. America has nearly become a kind of God, and the American way of Life a kind of religion. There is so much piety in Washington, DC, that a Church leader can get away with a God-is-dead declaration, while a president cannot survive without paying lip-service to a generalized American God. The religious sensitivity of the people becomes dull, and religion becomes a hand-maiden of the national purpose, and at times serves cheap, even immoral, political ends.[8]

On the other hand, Okite notes 'civil religion' such as that which has developed in America, enables people to give religious meaning to their history, and to relate national loyalty and identity to principles that are eternal and ultimate, and which transcend the nation and culture.

A development of this kind was lacking in the denominations which were founded in contemporary East Africa through the European missionary enterprise, because the Gospel was interpreted from the perspective of the missionaries. Africans were taught that their cultural and religious background was not only evil, but it was also uncivilized, savage, barbarian, and unworthy of a respectable human being. They were taught, therefore, to abandon their traditional way of life. Hence, the Africans recruited by missionaries into Christianity began to condemn the heritage of their own people, and to imitate the etiquette of missionaries. Those missionaries became not only evangelists, but also masters. In Embu in Eastern Kenya for example, the title which was used to address the missionary was the same as that used to describe the District Commissioner, and any other European. The Swahili title *Bwana* was used; in Embu it did not mean simply *Sister*, but *Master*. It is interesting to note that the same title, *Bwana* was used for African Protestant (Anglican) Clergymen in that area, and it continues to be used until this day.[9]

The rise of Independent Churches during the first half of the twentieth century in Kenya was an attempt not only to make a more relevant and meaningful expression of the Christian faith, but also to give religious meaning to the history of the people. The motif of the suffering children of Israel was very common, and the leaders of these Churches were symbolized as Moses, who delivered the children of Israel from bondage. The established Churches, by opposing the Independent Church Movement while at the same time tolerating imported denominations, betrayed themselves as supporters of the colonial powers. This is the way Africans saw it. Hence the African followers of the imported denominations, especially in Central Kenya, were considered to be betrayers of the struggle for independence, and many suffered during the struggle.

Okite, in an editorial in *Target* in 1974, argued that Independent Churches should be taken seriously because they have many lessons to teach the 'established Churches.' On the basis of the foregoing paragraphs, his argument and suggestions are worth following. He expounded them further in a public lecture at the University of Nairobi in January, 1975. The lecture was one in a series organized by the Department of Philosophy and Religious Studies, under the title *Christianity in Independent Africa*.[10]

Okite observed among other characteristics of Independent Churches that they are dynamic and lively, in contrast to the older denominations which adopted the liturgical forms of the 'mother Churches' in England, Scotland, Germany, and so on. The dullness which Okite observed in North America is largely present also in the denominations which were exported to Africa through the Missionary enterprise. This observation needs qualification, because those denominations are relevant and meaningful to the African worshippers. They have encouraged African Christians to compose local Christian songs, and the Roman Catholic Church has permitted the use of vernacular translations of the Bible whereas only the Latin text was permitted for many years.

Okite's sympathy for Independent Churches is not isolated. Many church leaders are realizing the ecumenical importance of these churches, and are willing to listen to what the leaders of those other churches have to say. Increasingly, the leaders of Independent Churches are also realizing that self-isolation is not in their interest and are applying for membership in ecumenical organizations such as the National Christian Council of Kenya, the All Africa

Conference of Churches and the World Council of Churches. Of the seven churches which were admitted to the Membership of the WCC during its Fifth General Assembly in Nairobi, three were Independent Churches, and two were Kenyan. The three were African Christian Church and Schools (Kenya), African Israel Church Nineveh (Kenya) and Church of the Lord (Aladura) from Nigeria. The African Church of the Holy Spirit was admitted into associate membership of the WCC.[12]

The term 'Independent Church' is rather vague in contemporary usage, because those churches that used to be run by missionary societies and agencies have now been handed over to African administrations. The leaders of these churches consider their denominations to be independent in the sense that they are autonomous bodies which are free to make their own policy decisions. At the same time, there are now missionary enterprises from North America and Western Europe, which have established themselves in East Africa within the past two decades, and are independent of the former Missionary Societies. In Kenya, for example, there are Churches founded by the Grace Independent Baptist Mission and these Churches are independent in a different sense from that of the category described above. Hence, there is a need to study the contemporary Church situation, and suggest more accurate classification.[13]

Kofi Appiah-Kubi has suggested that with regard to those that have been called 'Independent Churches' the most suitable label is 'Indigenous African Christian Churches.'[14] He suggests this title because, in his view, the main distinction between the established denominations and these Churches, is the fact that the latter were not extensions of Churches from abroad. Although all are African Christian Churches, the category in question has its roots in Africa, and its founders were African. The suggestion of Kofi Appiah-Kubi has not yet been widely accepted, but there is need to take it seriously. Joseph Kayo accepts this label, because his Church, though not independent in terms of relation between a mother-church and a daughter-church, it is indigenous in the sense that it has been founded by a Kenyan, and its members are African.

Odhiambo Okite calls for a new style of mission, in which Africa and all other continents can participate with equal effectiveness. This requires a more effective sharing of experiences in Christ throughout the world.[15] This style will involve the parishes all over the world to make efforts to learn what is happening in other parts of the world, and to appreciate the joys and sorrows of Christians across national boundaries, continental blocks, and cultural frontiers.

Another opportunity for doing foreign mission today is by recognizing the interrelatedness of our world and 'living in our local situations for our brother.' Unfortunately, Okite laments, North Americans have greater opportunities 'for living for us in Africa than we have for living for them. The power structure of our world makes influence flow in one direction, from them to us.'[16]

Okite calls for concern among all Christians to feel concerned about the welfare of all humanity so that pressing for 'fair prices for drugs and medical supplies' should be seen as an important Christian duty. Such an action, Okite suggests may have a greater impact on the health of our people than building church hospitals which are difficult and cumbersome to run. There is need, Okite points out, to educate the local Christians at the parish level, so that they understand their role as committed Christians and citizens in their village, district and nation, and as members of this interrelated and interdependent contemporary world. At the present time the majority of the laity are still ignorant of what is happening nationally and internationally, and the church leadership should consider it an important responsibility to educate the laity.

> The frontiers of Mission in North America . . . lie 'under water'! For the Church to do mission locally, it must go under. How else will it understand and relate effectively to the historical experiences of the Blacks and Natives? What about the Hispanic peoples on the farms of California? What has this Christian continent done to these people, and what can Christianity possibly mean for them after all that? Black and Red Theologies are the under-water theologies that are helping to liberate the American Church from its guilt, giving it a new vision for a new future as one people 'under God.'[17]

Though Odhiambo Okite does not state it explicitly, his argument applies to the contemporary East African situation. His sympathy for Indigenous African Christian Churches is a suggestion that the older imported denominations need to go 'under water' in order to become relevant and meaningful to the local people in the rural areas. Just as Black and Red Theologies have a significant role in the North American context, African Christian Theology in contemporary East Africa has a significant role in helping African Christians to realize that they can be committed Christians without having to imitate the cultural norms of a foreign people. The Christian Gospel challenges every culture including European and North American cultures.

Whereas the Gospel challenges and makes demands on Africans and their cultural backgrounds, there is no biblical justification for Christians of one race or tradition to impose their culture on the Christians of another. The arguments and premises for African Christian Theology have been outlined in a growing body of scholarship since the 1970s. In contemporary East Africa, the writings of Charles Nyamiti,[18] and Aylward Shorter[19] are useful for introductory reading with reference to the Roman Catholic Church. The publication *African and Black Theology*[20] also contains essays and discussions which emphasize the need for African Christians to express their commitment to the faith in terms which are relevant to their own existential context. My book *African Christian Theology: An Introduction* also contribute to the theme.[21]

Okite calls for a new type of Church. Only a new type of Church will be able to undertake a new type of mission, according to his suggestions which have been discussed above.[22] The new Church should be one which is willing to concentrate its concerns on the local people, the laity who are often under-privileged, misrepresented and ignorant. A Church which seeks to raise the welfare of the powerless, will be able to give new meaning to the concept of mission. Okite's call for a new type of Church, is in agreement with several participants of the World Council of Churches Fifth Assembly. Justice Jiagge of Ghana called for a new World Economic Order, which would shift the balance of influence from the consumers of the worlds's natural resources, to the producers. At present, she noted, seventy per cent of the world's natural resources are controlled and consumed by only thirty per cent of the world's population, concentrated mainly in Western Europe and North America. The remaining thirty per cent of the world's natural resources are shared by seventy per cent of the world's population. Can the Church remain silent about such a situation? Okite says no to this question, and suggests that the Church ought to play its role in trying to change this situation for the better.[23]

Thus Odhiambo Okite warns against Christianity being subordinated to the level of an instrument of the state. At the same time, he sees a positive role in Christianity, if those who are committed to it accept the challenge of making our contemporary world a more comfortable place to live in through sharing resources and experiences in Christ. Okite's suggestions are, in his view, additions to the existing efforts in mission, and not replacements of these efforts.

In his writings and addresses Okite has expressed his views on various aspects of Christianity within the context of contemporary East Africa, including the significance of Independent Churches, the need to take African religious heritage seriously, the necessity for the established Churches to renew their new lives and witness so that they may become new Churches with a commitment to do a new kind of mission. In his involvement in the development of Christian Education Curriculum in Kenya during 1970 and 1971, when he was co-chairman of the Joint Secondary School Panel, these concerns were often highlighted.

However, Okite's call for a new kind of Church and a new kind of mission, is based on his observation that the world has become a 'global village' in which nations and societies can no longer isolate themselves from each other. Technology has made all forms of physical communication very efficient, so that from Nairobi, for example, it is possible for a person to speak to another, instantaneously, through telephone and satellite communication links with most parts of the world. From Nairobi it is possible to travel by air to most parts of the world, and faster aircraft are being developed at a very high rate. The once marvellous Jumbo Jet was overtaken by the Supersonic Concorde, which in turn, has been superceded by re-used spacecraft Computers are making work much faster, and calculations more accurate. Nevertheless, this great advancement in technology is no guarantee that there will be closer understanding between nations, and from one society to another. The advancement of technology seems to apply even in the development of weapons, and the threat of war seems to be looming in every area of the world, as the most powerful compete for military, naval and nuclear supremacy. Each nation in the contemporary world seems to be keen to establish its remarkable impact among all others. The Churches' communities of peoples who are at the same time citizens of their nations, are caught up in these complicated frictions, competitions and conflicts.

When Okite supports the suggestion of 'ecumenical sharing of personnel,' he does not seem to take into serious account the fact that Christians as individuals have to act within the limits of the laws of their own nations, and this makes it difficult to generalize the principle of ecumenical sharing. Further, many Christians live in the countries which depend greatly on foreign aid and loans. The problem of theological education is that contemporary colleges in Africa have not established an African staff and continue to be run by missionaries, in spite of the loud and urgent call for the Africanization of theological education for contextual relevance and for the making of African Churches self-supporting, self-governing and self-propagating. However, the churches which sponsor the missionary teachers seem to be reluctant to spend the same money on African staff. They offer their financial aid provided that it is used to pay their own missionaries. The Africans who may qualify to teach in those institutions are expected to be paid by their own rural congregations, which are in fact unable to feed themselves adequately. These qualified Africans, who are often trained in Europe and America, find it difficult to work under those difficult conditions, and are forced to leave to seek employment elsewhere. The donor-churches abroad deal with this problem by exporting another missionary to replace the African who has resigned, and paying him with their aid. Such aid is not aid at all, in my opinion, it is an opportunity for these donor-churches to alleviate their unemployment problems at home.

Aid from the donor-churches in Europe and America, tends to be conditioned by terms dictated by the donors in the sameway as the aid and loans provided by secular agencies and governments. When Odhiambo Okite supports the proposal of Ecumenical sharing of personnel, he does not elaborate on how this vicious circle may be broken. It seems to me that the Churches with surplus incomes in Europe and America, just like their corresponding governments and business corporations, have to recognize the fact that they have accumulated their surplus through direct or indirect exploitation of the peoples of the so-called 'Third World.' If they acknowledge this fact, then they ought to proceed to the next step according to the teaching of Jesus — to share not just their surplus, but all they have, with those who have less or nothing. Only this kind of openness can make Okite's suggestion practicable. Nevertheless, the Churches alone cannot implement the proposal effectively, unless they convince the other institutions in their countries to follow this example, for the sake of a more humane and just society.

NOTES

1. Odhiambo Okite, 'Guest Editorial,' *International Review of Mission*, April 1974, p. 160.
2. ibid. p. 154.
3. ibid. p. 156.
4. David B Barret, *Schism and Renewal in Africa*, Oxford, 1968. Okite, *op. cit.* pp. 156-158.
5. Okite, *op. cit.* pp. 156-58.
6. Se *Kenya Churches Handbook*, p. 160.
7. Okite, *op. cit.* p. 158.
8. ibid. p. 157.
9. This title was used when addressing the settlers, the colonial administrators and all those who were in authority, so it acquired a different connotation from the common Swahili usage. In Tanzania the title seems to have been abandoned, possibly owing to such negative connotations, and the title *Ndugu* (Brother) is now used there.
10. The lectures were presented by J Donders, Samuel Kibicho, Odhiambo Okite and Judith Mbula.
11. The second Vatican Council (1962-65) removed this restriction, and the Mass is now said in the different local languages. See Walter M. Abott, *The Documents of Vatican II*, London: Geoffrey Chapman, 1966, p. 150.
12. WCC 5th Assembly, Nairobi: Plenary Document No. P D 6 23 November to 10 December, 1975.
13. Joe Kayo, Founder and Head of Deliverance Church, prefers the term *Indigenous Church*.
14. He maintained this view in the *Consultation on Independent Churches*, Nairobi: AACC Training Centre, 29-31 August, 1975.
15. Okite, *op. cit.* p. 158.
16. ibid. p. 159.
17. ibid. p. 160.
18. For example: Charles Nyamiti, *African Theology: Its Nature, Problems and Methods*, Gaba Pastoral Paper No. 19, Kampala, 1971, *The Scope of African Theology*, Kampala: Gaba Publications, 1973.

19. For example, Aylward Shorter, *African Theology,* London: Geoffrey Chapman, 1975, *African Culture and the Christian Church,* London: Geoffrey Chapman, 1974.
20. See Chapter Three above, note 69.
21. J.N.K. Mugambi, *African Christian Theology: An Introduction,* Nairobi: Heinemann 1989. See also my other books: *The Biblical Basis of Evangelization,* Nairobi: Oxford University Press, 1989; *African Heritage and Contemporary Christianity,* Nairobi: Longman, 1989.
22. Okite, op, cit. p. 156.
23. ibid, pp. 159-160. See also Richard D N Dickson, *To Set at Liberty the Oppressed,* Geneva: WCC Publication 1975; Marion Gallis, *Trade for Justice: Myth or Mandate,* Geneva: WCC Publication, 1972.

CONCLUSION

There is no doubt that Christianity, through the Euro-American missionary enterprise, has been the largest single factor which has contributed to the disruption of the social order and religious heritage of African peoples. Academic Education was for a long time managed and controlled by the missionary agencies, and through this formal education, Africans were taught to abandon or look down upon their heritage. In contemporary East Africa, many people who have gone through that missionary indoctrination are questioning the validity and motives of the missionary enterprise. This questioning logically leads to a questioning of the Christian Gospel itself.

Very few academically educated East Africans have concerned themselves with a deep analysis of the teaching of Jesus, from the Biblical perspective. Most of the criticism which has been launched against Christianity in East Africa, has been based on what the missionaries presented as Gospel of Jesus Christ. There is a need to reassess the missionary enterprise against the synoptic teaching of Jesus, and such a reassessment may contribute to an understanding of how far the missionary enterprises were within or outside the mandate of the Christian Gospel.

There has been little or no distinction between the *essence* of the Christian faith, and the *expression* of that faith. It seems that the essence of the faith is to be found in the Gospels. Other books of the Bible help to give the background of the life and teaching of Jesus, and the Epistles help to illustrate how the new teaching was implemented. Hence the Gospel provides basic principles which every individual and every community that accepts Jesus as Christ must translate into concrete action. Nevertheless, the contemporary East African interpretations of Christianity have not made this distinction. This is an aspect which may need more discussion in future, among both the advocates of Christianity and its critics.

Christianity in contemporary East Africa is a concern not only of clergymen and other Church leaders. It is also of serious concern to politicians, creative writers, artists, sociologists, political scientists, medical doctors and so on. The contemporary East African interpretations of Christianity must, therefore, be studied under an approach which brings all those involved in these disciplines and professions and interests into dialogue with one another. This study has been a preliminary attempt in this direction, and the insights gained during the study have been very rewarding. The teaching of contemporary interpretations of Christianity is crucial to the development of an East African Christian Theology, and to the discussion about the role of Christianity in East Africa's development. Professionals ought not to restrict their interpretations of Christianity to their own professions. They ought to share their insights with those concerned about the subject in other disciplines, so that they may influence each other, and help the younger generations to appreciate the relevant issues of their day.

Christianity has been understood to be a foreign religion by many East Africans. The slogan which was common in Central Kenya, that there was no difference between a missionary priest and any other European, was a statement of resentment which was coined when Africans realized that the conduct of some missionaries was not in the practical interests of the Africans. At the intellectual level, Kihumbu Thairu has raised fundamental questions which imply doubts on the validity of Christianity as a universal religion. John Mbiti, on the other hand, has made assertions which place Christianity above all other religions and claims Christianity to be indigenous to Africa.

It is necessary to distinguish Christianity as it is expressed in social structures, and Christianity as a set of principles derived from Jesus. As a social institution the Church was exported to Africa by missionary agencies of Christianity. If Christianity is defined as the way in which men and women in community should conduct themselves, one to another and in relation to God, it cannot be said to be completely alien to African culture and religion. Though Africans may not have known anything about Jesus before the missionary enterprise, they nevertheless knew the principle of 'loving your neighbour as yourself.' The foreignness or indigeneity of Christianity, therefore, needs further analysis and discussion.

One of the difficulties with Christianity is that it is based on the individual's commitment to, and faith in, Jesus Christ. This is its strength, but in another sense, it is its greatest weakness. If a person declares himself a Christian, it is not possible for any other human being to assess whether that declaration is genuine or not.

Contemporary East Africans have no way of concluding decisively that certain missionaries were or were not genuine in their missionary work. Only God can make such decisive judgement. Yet, at the same time, the failure of those who claim to be Christians to fulfil the claims of the Gospel, makes those to whom Christianity is proclaimed, suspicious of the missionaries. The Gospel claims to preach Good News to the poor, set at liberty the oppressed, and restore sight to the blind. If a missionary is not involved in the struggle of the oppressed for their own liberation, then the genuinness of his or her mission is doubted by those who are expected to accept it. This has been the basis for the criticism against the missionary enterprise in Africa.

Within contemporary East Africa there is a very wide variety of the expressions of Christianity. This variety, which sometimes leads to open conflicts especially in the rural areas, is scandalous for a faith which at the same time claims to be universal. The International Council of Christian Churches, whose membership is made up of very fundamentalist small churches held its ninth Congress at the Kenyatta Conference Centre in Nairobi, during August, 1975. The Conference was by some Kenyan Churches which belonged to the East African Christian Alliance. The World Council of Churches' Fifth Assembly was held at the same venue in November of the same year. The hosts were the WCC member Churches in Kenya. Clearly, both these organizations were antagonistic to each other. The ICCC always schedules meetings to counter those of the WCC throughout the world.

Although Christianity claims to have a universal appeal to all humanity, in contemporary East Africa, it has not proved to be beyond tribalism and racialism. In Uganda, this has been much more explicit than anywhere else in East Africa. But this is not to suggest that tribalism has not been a notable factor in the expression of Christianity in other parts. The difficulty of language already imposes division along ethnic lines, and language, being one of the avenues for the transmission of culture, has led to an interesting phenomeon. Kiswahili, English and local languages are used all at the same time, depending on the needs of the members of a particular congregation or parish. Can Christianity be a unifying factor without other more basic elements of culture such as language, education, and aesthetic values? I doubt it, unless Christian unity is accepted only at the spiritual level. Yet, the affirmation of unity through Christian spirituality should bring about reconciliation, and co-operation at the social, economic, political, ethical and aesthetic levels. Otherwise such affirmation would be practically irrelevant.

At the theological level, contemporary interpretations of Christianity have not been very detailed. The traditional doctrinal debates of Western Christendom have not been the centre of concern in contemporary East Africa. The discussion among both Christians and non-Christians has tended to concentrate on the cultural impact of Euro-American Christianity on the traditional African communities. It seems that a deeper theological debate could raise these perennial issues again more sharply. But it is Africans themselves who have to respond to the Gospel and to the Church in East Africa, and influence one another as they search for a more satisfying expression of faith, and a more effective strategy for the enhancement of peace, love and unity for all people. The question raised and documented by Albert Schweitzer, for example, seems to be important as a theological springboard: What is the relationship between the Jesus of History and the Christ of Faith? What is the implication of this relationship for the contemporary East African situation? These are questions which African Christians must answer for themselves, and to which the critics of Christianity also, ought to respond.

In the context of contemporary East Africa, Professor Donders has summarized the situation in a short sermon, which is concerned with the same subject that this study has attempted to analyse in detail. His words seem appropriate in this conclusion.

My "Old boys"
from very devout African Christian schools remain
brave followers of Jesus Christ.
Others, however,
are very outspoken
In their refusal of that same Jesus of Nazareth.

Their reasons are often the same
They say and write things like

Jesus is a stranger in Africa,
He is an expatriate,
He comes from another world.
He is a product of the west
He is an imperialist
He is a colonialist
He is pretentious.

You cannot be faithful to African Culture and obey him;
You cannot be yourself as an African
and be a Christian
He is an alienator

It is very true to say
that Jesus is a stranger,
to many,
maybe even to all of us
He is a Jew
He is an Asian
From Asia Minor
but nevertheless from Asia

He lived there 2000 years ago
in a completely different situation.

He really is a stranger
but, if you believe in Him,
then it must have been you
who recognized something in Him.
And if this recognition comes from you,
how could it be strange to you?

That is what happened to the two friends from Emmaus.
Jesus did not reveal Himself
He took bread,
He broke it

and they recognized Him
Him, the bread-breaker
the universal companion!

The debate about the relevance of Christianity in contemporary and future East Africa will continue. While the critics continue to expose the weakness of this religion and the shortcomings of its witnesses, the number of converts continues to rise, and the rate of growth is higher in the Independent Churches whose founders and followers are also, like the critics, uncomfortable with the Churches originally introduced by European and American missionaries. Christianity is in East Africa to stay, but its contribution to the constructive development of society will depend very much on the continuation of constructive debate between the critics and the apologists of this religion. Hopefully, willingness and openness will grow among all those concerned (negatively or positively) with religion, to meet and challenge each other constructively, so that Christians, ex-Christians and non-Christians may learn from, and correct each other, for mutual understanding.

BIBLIOGRAPHY

Abbot, Walter M, ed. *The Documents of Vatican II*, London: Geoffrey Chapman, 1966

Adler, EA *Small Beginning: An Assessment of the First Five Years of the Programme to Combat Racism*, Geneva: WCC, 1974

Agbeti, *JK*, *'African Theology: What It Is,'* in presence, Vol. V No. 3, 1972, Geneva: WSCF Atieno-Odhiambo, ES, *The Paradox of Collaboration and Other Essays*, Nairobi: East African Literature Bureau, 1974

Barrett, DB, *Schism and Renewal*, London: Oxford University Press, 1968

—, ed, *African Initiatives in Religion*, Nairobi: East African Publishing House, 1971

—, ed, *Kenya Churches Handbook*, Kisumu, Kenya: Evangel Press, 1975

—, ed, *World Christian Encyclopaedia*, Nairobi: Oxford University Press, 1981

Beard, Ruth M, *An Outline of Piaget's Development Psychology*, London: Routledge and Kegan Paul, 1969

Carpenter, GW, *The Way in Africa*, London: Edinburgh House Press, 1960

Carr, Burgess, 'Moratorium: The Search for Authenticity,' in *AACC Bulletin*, May-June 1974

—, The Engagement of Lusaka,' in *Official Report of the Third Assembly of the All Africa Conference of Churches*, Nairobi: 1974

Cone, JH, *Black Theology and Black Power*, New York: Seabury Press, 1969

—, *A Black Theology of Liberation*, Philadelphia: Lippincott, 1970

—, *The Spirituals and the Blues*, New York: Seabury Press, 1972

—, *God of the Oppressed*, New York: Seabury Press, 1975.

Dain, R and Jac Van Diepen, *Luke's Gospel for African Today*, Nairobi: Oxford University Press, 1972

Dickinson, RDN, *To Set at Liberty the 'Oppressed*, Geneva: WCC, 1975

—, *Poor, Yet Making Many Rich*, Geneva: WCC, 1983

Dickson, Kwesi, *Theology in Africa*, Maryknoll, New York: Orbis, 1984

Dickson K and Paul Ellingworth, eds, *Biblical Revelation and African Beliefs*, London: Lutterworth, 1969

Donders, JG, *Expatriate Jesus and Other Sermons*, Nairobi: Gazelle Books, 1975

—, *Don't Fence Us In: The Liberating Power of Philosophy*, Inaugural Lecture, University of Nairobi, 1975

—, *Non Bourgeois Theology*, Maryknoll, New York: Orbis, 1986

Elders and Deacons of Nairobi Baptist Church, *Jesus Christ Frees and Unites: A Response to Preparatory Documents of the WCC 5th Assembly*, Nairobi, 1975

Fashole' Luke, EW, 'The Quest for African Christian Theology,' Paper presented at the Ibadan Conference of the West African Association of Theological Institutions, September, 1974

First, Ruth, *The Barrel of a Gun*, Harmondsworth: Penguin, 1970

Fisher, HAL, *A History of Europe, Vol. I, From the Earliest Times to 1713*, London: Collins Fontana, 1935

Gallis, Marion, *Trade for Justine: Myth or Mandate?* Geneva: WCC, 1972

Gatu, John, 'Opening Sermon' in *Official Report of the Fourth Assembly of the All Africa Conference of Churches*, Nairobi: AACC, 1982

Hastings, A, *Christian Marriage in Africa*, London: SPCK, 1973

Hordern, W, *A Layman's Guide to Protestant Theology*, New York: Macmillan, 1957

Kaggia, B, *Roots of Freedom*, Nairobi: East African Publishing House, 1975

Kato, B, *Theological Pitfalls in Africa*, Nairobi: Evangel Press, 1975

Kenyatta, J, *Facing Mount Kenya*, London: Secker and Warburg, 1938

Kibicho, SG, 'The Continuity of the African Conception of God into and Through Christianity, with the Kikuyu Conception of "Ngai" as a Case Study,' Seminar Paper, Nairobi, 14 January, 1975

Kieran, J, 'The Holy Ghost Fathers in East Africa,' Thesis, University of London, 1966

King, KJ and AI Salim, eds, *Kenya National Biographies*, Nairobi: East African Publishing House, 1971

Kinyanjui, Kabiru, *Struggle with God*, Kampala: Sapoba Bookshop Press, 1985

—, 'Justice, Peace and Reconciliation: The Challenge to the Church Today,' in S Kobia and G Ngumi, eds, *Together in Hope: Official Report of the Mission Conference 1989*, Nairobi: NCCK, 1991

—, 'Development, Social Justice and the Church,' Seminar Paper delivered at the NCCK Staff Consultation, Limuru Kenya, 6 February, 1975

Kipkorir, BE, 'The Alliance High School and the Formation of the Elite in Kenya,' Thesis, Cambridge University, 1970

Kiwanuka, MSM, *From Colonialism to Independence*, Nairobi: East African Literature Bureau, 1973

—, 'Uganda Under the British,' in BA Ogot and JA Kieran, eds, *Zamani*, Nairobi: East African Publishing House, and Longman Kenya, 1969

Kofi Appiah-Kubi and Sergio Torres, eds, *African Theology en Route*, Maryknoll, New York: Orbis, 1979

Long, Charles, *Significations: Signs, Symbols and Images in the Interpretation of Religion*, Philadelphia: Fortress Press, 1986

Mambo, G, 'The Revival Fellowship in Kenya,' in DB Barrett and others, eds, *Kenya Churches Handbook*, Kisumu, Kenya: Evangel Press, 1974

Mazrui, Ali, 'Aesthetic Dualism and Creative Literature in East Africa,' in Pio Zirimu and Andrew Gurr, eds, *Black Aesthetics*, Nairobi: East African Literature Bureau, 1973

Mbiti, JS, *African Religions and Philosophy*, London: Heinemann, 1969, 2nd ed, 1989

—, *Concepts of God in Africa*, London: SPCK, 1970

—, *The Crisis of Mission in Africa*, Mukono: Uganda Church Press, 1971

—, *New Testament Eschatology in an African Background*, Oxford: Clarendon Press, 1971

—, *Introduction to African Religion,* London: Heinemann, 1975

—, *Bible and Theology in African Christianity,* Nairobi: Oxford University Press, 1986

—, 'Church and State: A Neglected Element of Christianity in Contemporary Africa,' in *Africa Theological Journal,* No. 5, Dec., 1972

Mbula, Judith, *Our Religious Heritage,* London: Nelson, 1982

—, 'Penetration of Christianity in Ukambani,' Thesis, University of Nairobi, 1974

McVeigh, Malcolm, *God in Africa: Conceptions of God in African Traditional Religion and Christianity,* Cape Cod, Mass: Claude Stark, 1974

Moltmann, J, *The Crucified God,* London: SCM Press, 1973

Moore, Basil, ed, *Black Theology: The South African Voice,* London: Christopher Hurst, 1973

Mude Dae Mude, 'The Church and Traditional Africa,' Commentary, *The (Kenya) Standard,* 10 January, 1976

Muga, E, *African Response to Western Christian Religion,* Nairobi: East African Literature Bureau, 1975

Mugambi, JNK, *African Christian Theology: An Introduction,* Nairobi: Heinemann, 1989

—, *African Heritage and Contemporary Christianity,* Nairobi: Longman, 1989

—, *The Biblical Basis for Evangelization,* Nairobi: Oxford University Press, 1989

—, *God, Humanity and Nature,* Geneva: WCC, 1987

Mugo, MMG, *Visions of Africa,* Nairobi: East African Literature Bureau, 1978

Mutua, RW, *Development of Education in Kenya,* Nairobi: East African Literature Bureau, 1975

Ndingi, R, 'Church and State in Kenya,' in DB Barrett and others, eds, *Kenya Churches Handbook,* Kisumu, Kenya: Evangel Press, 1975

Ngugi wa Thing'o, *Weep Not, Child,* London: Heinemann, 1964

—, *The River Between,* London: Heinemann, 1965

—, *A Grain of Wheat,* London: Heinemann, 1968

—, *Homecoming,* London: Heinemann, 1972

—, *Secret Lives,* London: Heinemann, 1975

—, *Petals of Blood,* London: Heinemann, 1977

Nkrumah, Kwame, *Consciencism: Philosophy and Ideology for Decolonisation,* London: Panaf, 1964; Paperback edition 1970

Nyamiti, C, *African Thology: Its Nature, Problems and Methods,* Kampala: Gaba Publications, 1971

—, *The Scope of African Theology,* Kampala: Gaba Publications, 1973

Ochieng, WR, 'An Essay on Tribalism,' in *Joliso, Journal of Literature and Society,* Vol. I No. 1, 1972

—, 'Christianity and African Cultural Liberation,' in *Sunday Post,* Nairobi: 16 June, 1974

Ogot, BA, 'A Man More Sinned Against than Sinning — The African Writer' View of Himself,' in Pio Zirimu and Andrew Gurr, eds, *Black Aesthetics: Papers from a Coloquium at the University of Nairobi, June 1971,* Nairobi: East African Literature Bureau, 1973

Ogot, BA and JA Kieran, eds, *Zamani,* Nairobi: East African Publishing House and Longman Kenya, 1969

162

Okite, Odhiambo, 'Guest Editorial,' *International Review of Mission,* Geneva: WCC, April 1974

Okot p'Bitek, *Song of Lawino,* Nairobi; East African Publishing House, 1967

—, *Song of Ocol,* Nairobi: East African Publishing House, 1970

—, *African Religions in Western Scholarship,* Nairobi: East African Literature Bureau, 1970

—, *Religion of Central Luo,* Nairobi: East African Literature Bureau

—, *Song of Prisoner and Song of Malaya,* Nairobi: East African Publishing House, 1971

—, *Africa's Cultural Revolution,* London: Macmillan, 1973

Okullu, Henry, *Church and Politics in East Africa,* Nairobi; Uzima Press, 1974

—, *Church and State in Nation Building and Human Development,* Nairobi: Uzima, 1984

Oliver, Roland, *The Missionary Factor in East Africa,* London: Longman, 1952, New Impression 1970

Olsen, H, *African Myths about Christianity,* Kijabe, Kenya: AIC Press, 1972

Russell, B, *Why I Am Not a Christian,* London: Allen and Unwin, 1954

Shorter, Aylward, *The African Contribution to World Church and Other Essays,* Kampala: Gaba Publications, 1972

—, *African Culture and the Christian Church,* London: Chapman, 1973

—, *African Christian Theology,* London: Chapman, 1975

—, *Toward a Theology of Inculturation,* London: Chapman, 1988

Shorter, Aylward and Kataza, eds, *Missionaries to Yourselves,* London: Chapman, 1975

Smith, EW and AM Dale, *The Ila-Speaking Peoples of Northern Rhodesia, Vol. I,* London: Edinburgh House Press, 1920

Smoker, DE, 'Decision Making in East African Revival Movement Groups,' in DB Barrett, ed, *African Initiative in Religion,* Nairobi: East African Publishing House, 1971

Sundermeier, Theo, ed, *Church and Nationalism in South Africa,* Johannesburg: Ravan Press, 1975

Taban Lo Liyong, *The Last Word,* Nairobi: East African Publishing House, 1967

—, *Thirteen Offensives Against Our Enemies,* Nairobi: East African Literature Bureau, 1973

—, *Culture is Rutan,* Nairobi: Longman, 1991

Taylor, JV, *The Primal Vision,* London: SCM Press, 1963

Tempels, Placide, *Bantu Philosophy,* Paris: Presence Africaine, 1959

Temu, AJ, *Protestant Missions in East Africa,* London: Longman, 1973

—, 'British Protestant Missions on the Kenya Coast and Highlands,' Thesis, University of Alberta, 1967

Thairu, K, *Afrikan Civilization,* Nairobi: East African Literature Bureau, 1975

Vaughan, BNY, *The Expectation of the Poor: The Church in the Third World,* London: SCM Press, 1972

Verkuyl, J, *Break Down the Walls: A Christian Cry for Racial Justice,* Grand Rapids, Mich: Eerdmans, 1973

Weiland, JS, *New Ways in Theology,* Dublin: Gill and Macmillan, 1968

Welbourn, FB., *East African Christian,* London: Oxford University Press, 1965

—, *Religion and Politics in Uganda,* Nairobi: East African Publishing House, 1965

Were, GS and D Wilson, *East Africa Through a Thousand Years*, Ibadan: Evans Brothers, 1968; 2nd ed, 1972

Zirimu, Pio and Andrew Gurr, eds, *Black Aesthetics: Papers from the Colloquium Held at the University of Nairobi, June 1971*, Nairobi: East African Literature Bureau, 1973

164

INDEX

166

Piaget, Jean 37
Presbyterian Church 71, 109, 137
protestant Churches 8, 14, 20, 35, 44, 71

Reformation, Protestant iii, 10, 147
Revivalists 109-112
Robinson, John A T 13
Roman Catholic Church iii, 7, 14, 23, 31
   n.18, 35, 45, 55, 71, 149, 151
Roman Empire iii, 72
Rwanda 109
Russell, Bertrand 13

Schelling, Friedrich 21
Schweitzer, Albert 160
Shorter, Aylward 4, 40-46, 151
slave trade 29
Smith, Edwin 8, 9
Southall, Aidan 86-87
syncretism 5-6, 44, 62

Taylor, John V 1, 37, 39-40
technology, influence of 13, 24-26, 152-153
Tempels, Placide 11, 43

Temple, Frederick 23
Temu, A J 26, 33
Thairu, Kuhumbu 71-73, 157
time, concepts of 9, 68, 73-76
tribalism 57, 58-60, 158

Uganda 11, 12, 15, 34-35, 45-46, 54, 109,
   158
Uhuru 53, 87, 90, 92, 96-97, 118, 131, 138-
   139

Van Buren, Paul 13

Wallace, A R 21
Warren, M A C 86
Washington, Booker T 24-25
Welbourn, F B 34-39, 83, 85
Williams, Eric 29
World Council of Churches 16, 62, 133,
   141, 150, 152, 158